FIGHTING THE GOOD FIGHT

FIGHTING THE GOOD FIGHT

Why On-Ice Violence is Killing Hockey

Adam Proteau

WILEY

John Wiley & Sons Canada, Ltd.

Library and Archives Canada Cataloguing in Publication
Proteau, Adam
    Fighting the good fight : why on-ice violence is killing hockey
/ Adam Proteau.

Issued also in electronic formats.
ISBN 978-1-118-09222-4

    1. Hockey.   2. Violence in sports.   I. Title.

GV847.P735 2011   796.962   C2011-902686-4

ISBN 978-1-118-09222-4 (paper); 978-1-118-09492-1 (Mobi); 9781118094938 (ePDF); 978-1-118-09489-1 (ePub)

Production Credits
Cover Design: Adrian So
Cover Photo Credit: © istockphoto/Thinkstock
Composition: Thomson Digital
Printer: Solisco Tri-Graphic Printing Ltd.

Editorial Credits
Executive Editor: Karen Milner
Production Editor: Pauline Ricablanca

John Wiley & Sons Canada, Ltd.
6045 Freemont Blvd.
Mississauga, Ontario
L5R 4J3

Printed in Canada
1 2 3 4 5 SOL TRI 15 14 13 12 11

ENVIRONMENTAL BENEFITS STATEMENT

John Wiley & Sons - Canada saved the following resources by printing the pages of this book on chlorine free paper made with 100% post-consumer waste.

TREES	WATER	ENERGY	SOLID WASTE	GREENHOUSE GASES
45	43847	70	5543	14408
FULLY GROWN	GALLONS	MILLION BTUs	POUNDS	POUNDS

CONTENTS

*To fight and conquer in all your battles is not supreme
excellence; supreme excellence consists in breaking
the enemy's resistance without fighting.*
—Sun Tzu, Chinese philosopher and
author of *The Art of War*

Fighting for peace is like screwing for virginity.
—George Carlin, comedian and social critic

THE BEATINGS

AND THE DAMAGE DONE
THE SORRY STATE OF TODAY'S NHL

The 1972 Summit Series that pitted Canada against the Soviet Union is one of the most seminal moments in the history of hockey. And in that series, one of the heroes for the Canadian team was a gap-toothed, maple-syrup-bleeding, 23-year-old whirling dervish named Bobby Clarke.

Clarke's biggest contribution to that Summit Series tourna-ment—won, of course, by Canada in a come-from-behind, eight-game victory—did not take the form of a goal scored, a deft assist, or a soul-stirring locker-room intermission speech.

Instead, a large part of Clarke's legacy was forged forever in Game 6 of the Summit Series, when he swung his stick down on the ankle of Valeri Kharlamov and fractured the Soviet star forward's ankle, essentially leaving the Russian star a shell of himself for the rest of his career.

Clarke, meanwhile, went on to enjoy a 15-year career in the National Hockey League (NHL), win two Stanley Cups with the infamously over-aggressive "Broad St. Bully" Philadelphia Flyers, and retire as a first-ballot Hockey-Hall-of-Famer. Indeed, Clarke embodied the win-at-all-costs mentality that had a stranglehold on elite-level North American hockey long before then—and that still carries sway in the NHL.

Today, even Bobby Clarke thinks things have gone too far and the costs are too high.

Now a 62-year-old executive with the Flyers, Clarke recognizes what most of us who've watched the hockey world recognize: the NHL—the sport's standard-bearer—is increasingly becoming a league in which the primary goal for its players has shifted from contesting a game to, in reality, surviving it.

As Clarke has noted on numerous occasions, the NHL is long beyond the point where players employ a body check to separate a member of the opposing team from the puck. Now, NHLers are instructed to use themselves as wrecking balls laying waste to the other side, regardless of the consequences for their opponents—or themselves and their own bodies.

"You used to hit to separate a guy from the puck," Clarke told me on the set of TSN's *Off The Record* program. "Nowadays, it seems like players hit to separate their opponent's head from his body."

Players have also been emboldened by state-of-the-art protection from Kevlar equipment that could stop a bazooka attack from point-blank range and, at the same time, be used to further decimate the bodies and brains of on-ice adversaries. Player equipment has become as much about protecting the athlete as it is about emboldening them into feeling bulletproof on the ice. As well, modern-day players are far different from their predecessors in that current NHLers use their hard-shell elbow and shoulder pads to obliterate an opponent.

In fact, if the league's worker-bee players don't "finish their checks"—hockey code for, "launch your body fully and completely into the rat bastard on the other side"—management usually replaces them with "high-energy players" (another hockey euphemism for "encouraged line-crossers") from the minor leagues who are willing to play with an extreme level of aggression in exchange for a healthier paycheck.

More than a quarter-century after Clarke stopped playing in 1984, and due to a variety of factors we'll examine throughout this book, for the sport's best players, the game of hockey is now more dangerous than ever before. Concussions are threatening to end the careers of some of the NHL's best players—including Sidney Crosby, the league's biggest marquee superstar—and a significant percentage of all NHLers are dealing with head injuries. While advances in medicine and science offer us better indications of the toll taken on athletes in high-impact sports, and while medical officials still speak out against the lack of sufficient player protection in hockey, the best hockey league in the world has simply not moved quickly enough.

The NHL's approach to player safety can correctly be called cavalier, but—make no mistake—the league isn't run by a loose-knit collection of wealthy sadists who are simply in it for the kicks that come with being part of a pseudo Fight Club.

No, theirs (and by theirs, I mean the NHL team owners who tell league president Gary Bettman what to do) is a highly calculated, profit-driven philosophy: a delicate balancing act in which the league must present the appearance it cares while, at the same time, promoting a hyper-aggressive style of play that leads directly to players suffering grievous injuries.

Why do Bettman and the owners try and have it both ways on the issue of violence? For the same reason each and every fast-food store drains small silos of salt in preparing their product: they simply don't believe it will sell without it. Similarly, although fighting and senseless aggressiveness are as unhealthy for hockey as a double Big Mac dipped in lard and formaldehyde is to the average human heart, the NHL operates under the assumption that fighting must be included with the actual on-ice product to make it more palatable for the masses.

In other words, the NHL has no faith in its core product. The NHL markets illegal acts—because don't forget, all fights are against the rules. Go to www.nhl.com during the regular season and you'll see enforcers and fisticuffs in the main news story rotation. Now try and think of another reputable sports league that would do such a thing. You'll be thinking a long, long time.

• • •

This leads us to the product the NHL puts on the ice today. To be sure, every game played under the league's banner is as much a product as any dish soap or toothpaste; those who consume the product come to expect things in return for their money. Any NHL fan has expectations of seeing: (a) a game played and won (which wasn't always the case when the NHL allowed games to end in ties); and (b) enough entertainment and excitement to justify what have grown to become highly unjustifiable ticket prices. Beyond that, though, the product— in terms of the style of hockey that's presented—is entirely up to those who administrate the sport.

And the NHL's modern-day product essentially was formed after the 2004–05 lockout season, a disgrace of a labor war propagated by Bettman under the guise of league-wide parity, that was, in reality, an exercise in cost control and boosting the value of franchises. One of the very few good things to come out of the lost season was the opportunity for the league to examine what its game had become. And what it had become was a dreary, low-scoring, predictable display of defense-first hockey that pleased only coaches and goalies.

So when the chance came to make changes to the game, a group of progressive-minded members of the NHL community (led by former Detroit Red Wings star and current NHL vice-president of hockey and business development Brendan Shanahan) jumped on it, redefining what hockey could be—a fast, physical feast for the eyes that stressed skill and speed rather than a game that had become known for inhibiting skill and promoting a plodding, ponderous pace.

Sure enough, that's precisely what hockey became again, to the delight of fans and media who had grown tired of what became known as the Dead Puck Era. But one of the biggest unintended consequences of the positive changes (essentially, a full-on crackdown on obstruction) was the increased speed of the players; it allowed the team with puck possession to move unimpeded through the neutral zone and crash down on the defending players once they collapsed inside their blue line.

All in all, the changes took an already-physical NHL game and made it into a season-long Thunderdome of sorts, where mere survival from night to night, week to week, and year to year is as much of a goal as the display of offensive or defensive talent.

Let's stop and reflect on that for a second. In the NHL, it isn't enough anymore to be fantastically skilled at playing within the rules of the game; you also have to be adept at avoiding the league's designated decimators, the head-hunting players who exist solely to physically harm their opponents.

Contrast that conscious NHL management decision on player safety with those made by other professional sports leagues.

The National Football League (NFL)—by far the most successful of all pro leagues, with billions in revenue per season—has gone to great lengths to protect its quarterbacks (its most important players in both the competitive and marketing senses) by banning defensive players from potentially knocking QBs out of the lineup with cheap shots, late hits, hits to the head, and even hitting below the knees.

In rugby—one of the most violent, vicious sports anywhere on the planet—the sport's administrators tolerate none of the nonsense tolerated by the NHL. In 2005, a UK league player named Julian White was suspended for eight weeks for fighting—a suspension that included professional league games and extended to games representing his country—even though the three-member disciplinary panel accepted White's excuse that he was provoked and fought in self-defense.

Like the NFL, the National Basketball Association (NBA)—a more profitable business in the United States than the NHL—deals equally harshly with its players who overstep the boundaries of base-level sportsmanship and respect.

NBA commissioner David Stern has suspended superstar players such as Steve Nash not only for the regular season but also for the all-important and financially lucrative playoffs merely for leaving the bench during an on-court skirmish. Nash never threw a punch, never tried to bite another player. He merely left the bench to assist a teammate who was embroiled in a skirmish, yet was suspended anyway because the league he works for does not tolerate puffed-up macho nonsense.

When matters have really gotten out of hand in Stern's league—as they did in Detroit between the Pistons and the visiting Indiana Pacers in November 2004, when players fought each other as well as fans in the stands—Ron Artest, the main culprit involved, was suspended for 86 games (73 regular season games and 13 playoff games) while another player was suspended for 30 games.

There has not been another NBA fight in the stands since that night in Michigan.

Incredibly, some hockey traditionalists will hear that comparison, recognize the terrible light in which it casts the NHL's tepid attempts at controlling player behavior, and claim hockey is inherently different from football, rugby, or basketball, that the combination of speed on skates and ensuing collisions necessitates the use of fights and other assault-like actions.

The sport's traditionalists will argue over and over that hockey players are the toughest pro athletes anywhere—and in the same breath they'll tell you why hockey players simply can't "suck it up" and turn the other cheek on cheap shots, the way other athletes in collision sports do.

The sad fact is, hockey players don't need a cheap shot to go off. There aren't many things that take place in the game anymore that don't involve at least a scrum of players, a glove in the face, or a full-on punch at the tail end of it. Every hard body check thrown—whether clean, borderline, or outright dirty, whether thrown at and absorbed by a star player or a no-name call-up from the minor leagues—results in an escalation of aggressive tactics.

• • •

Is there anyone in the NHL community who can stomach all the on-ice shenanigans without lashing out? Sure. And for more than a decade, the most prominent league employee, after Bettman, was his director of hockey operations, Colin Campbell. Campbell recently relinquished his role as the league's chief disciplinarian, but from 1998 until June 2011, he was the man responsible for determining who committed a hockey crime and who was innocent of any wrongdoing.

It has never been wise to place all or even the majority of blame on Campbell, a former player and head coach who goes to great lengths to be fair (at least by NHL standards). He took direction from Bettman and the owners and was told to interpret a rulebook that is thousands of shades of gray instead of the standard black and white.

Nonetheless, to say Campbell's idea of justice is inconsistent is to say the prices of concession foods at movie theatres are slightly inflated. Campbell's verdicts are like snowflakes—none of them are ever the same, and each one has as much chance of leaving a lasting impression on the suspended player as does a tiny speck of half-frozen rain.

By and large, NHL suspensions come in three varieties. The first is the standard one-, two-, or three-game ban normally given to a first-time offender whose victim suffers only minor injuries (the league always takes into account the effect and not the intent of any action).

The second is the more serious four-to-six-game penalty given to repeat offenders and/or players whose victims suffer a more serious injury. An example of a four-to-six game penalty can be found in the 2010 exploits of Pittsburgh Penguins agitator Matt Cooke. One of the NHL's most-hated players, Cooke earned the eternal hatred of Boston Bruins fans in 2009–10 when he blindsided Bruins center Marc Savard with an elbow to the head that was neither whistled as a penalty nor cited as sufficient cause for an immediate and lengthy suspension. Savard returned in the post-season that year, but was sidelined, perhaps permanently, in February 2011 after suffering another serious concussion that left him dealing with memory problems and other cognitive afflictions. Meanwhile, in the 2010–11 season, the 32-year-old Cooke continued his over-the-borderline play; in consecutive games in February 2011, he was involved in what appeared to be an intentional knee-on-knee hit on Washington Capitals superstar Alex Ovechkin, then checked Columbus Blue Jackets defenseman Fedor Tyutin from behind and into the boards headfirst. Both Ovechkin and Tyutin escaped serious injury— but both could have had their careers end in an instant.

Cooke was not suspended for his hit on Ovechkin. On the Tyutin hit, he apparently crossed a line and was suspended. But get this: despite the fact that it was the third time Cooke had been suspended in his 12-year NHL career, and despite injuring Savard less than a year earlier, Cooke only received a four-game ban for the Tyutin hit.

A four-game suspension represents less than five percent of an 82-game regular season. Need anyone wonder why NHLers take revenge into their own hands? If players know the league will tacitly endorse over-the-top behavior by not levying serious suspensions, isn't their only choice to go vigilante on the guy who "deserved it"?

More importantly, guess what happened after that supposedly strict suspension for Cooke?

Yes, a mere month after his hits on Ovechkin and Tyutin, Cooke came across center ice during a game against the New York Rangers and, as he approached defenseman Ryan McDonagh, jutted out his elbow directly and intentionally into McDonagh's head.

• • •

That brings us to the third variety of NHL suspension: the very rare, double-digit ban handed out in egregious situations where the league cannot avoid serious scrutiny from non-hockey fans and the media.

Cooke's elbow on McDonagh came less than two weeks after the league's 30 GMs had met and, along with Bettman, put together a five-point plan to improve how the league addressed its treatment of the concussion issue. The five points included arena safety improvements, softer equipment, and tougher punishments for repeat offenders. Penguins owner and all-time hockey great Mario Lemieux suggested fines for teams who employ unnecessarily dangerous players—a move that showed leadership considering what he'd pay by having Cooke on the roster.

But here was Cooke, still making no effort to change his ways, still playing as if he had no fear the league would take away a significant portion of his salary, nor seemingly aware that he had devastated the career of Marc Savard, a former star whose career appears to be over in part because of Cooke's elbow. Cooke had been a player without a conscience in a league without a conscience, at least in terms of the price paid by its key employees. Why would he worry?

Unfortunately for Lemieux, public sentiment on Cooke's behavior had reached its nadir. Critics were openly taunting Lemieux, snidely supposing he and the Penguins organization would—as so many organizations had done before—turn a blind eye to their own player's vicious streak. But showing himself worthy of his earlier words, Lemieux and the Penguins applauded when the NHL reacted to public anger and suspended Cooke for the final 10 games of the 2010–11 regular season and the first round of the playoffs.

Another egregious incident happened in February 2004, when then–Vancouver Canucks winger Todd Bertuzzi punched Colorado Avalanche forward Steve Moore, then landed on top of him—breaking Moore's neck and triggering a lawsuit that had yet to be resolved by the time this book went to press. It's an incident we'll examine in greater detail later in the book.

The public outcry was loud and angry, and the NHL suspended Bertuzzi for the remainder of the 2003–04 campaign, and what it termed "indefinitely." Even then, the league's supplementary discipline department failed to rebuke Bertuzzi as harshly as the situation demanded. Bertuzzi sat out the rest of Vancouver's regular-season games—20 in total—and did not play a single game of hockey in the 2004–05 season. The thing is, very few NHLers played hockey that year—and definitely not in the NHL; remember, that was the season NHL team owners locked out Bertuzzi and the members of the National Hockey League Players' Association (NHLPA).

Now, you can argue that Bertuzzi could've done what some NHLers did during the lockout and play in a professional European league for a seven-figure salary. You'd also be right in saying Bertuzzi's penalty was not insignificant. He has paid a bigger price than many realize or admit. But there is no doubt that many hockey fans and players were disgusted to see Bertuzzi returning to the NHL to begin the 2005–06 season and remain disgusted to see him continue to play through the 2010–11 campaign, while Moore never played another game after being injured.

Through this saga, you can understand why players feel the need to exact their own revenge on the ice. The NHL's administrators certainly aren't looking out for them.

• • •

If you want to see where the NHL's priorities really lie in regard to player safety, you have to look at the recent suspension history of Sean Avery. Like Cooke of the Penguins, Avery's job on the ice is to be a pest—to get under his opponents' skin and sucker them into taking penalties. Avery is arguably the best hockey player in history at that job. As a matter of fact, he's too good at it—so good that he became one of the most loathed players (and not just among fans, but among his fellow NHLers) to play at hockey's best level. Avery does so by going where few players ever go: into his opponents' personal lives, ridiculing or otherwise infuriating them to the point they see red and retaliate physically.

Over his career, Avery had been accused of uttering racial slurs during a game and he'd had nasty run-ins with his own team's coaches and broadcaster. On the ice, he was notorious for goading opposing players into dropping their gloves to fight him, only to "turtle" (cover his head with his hands and refuse to fight). But in December 2008, Avery committed a sin that—to the hockey world—was worse than anything already on his rap sheet.

At the time, Avery was a member of the Dallas Stars and was in front of a group of media cameras in Calgary prior to a game against the Calgary Flames. Out of nowhere, and seemingly only to amuse himself, Avery began referring to a former girlfriend—Canadian actress Elisha Cuthbert, by then the girlfriend of Flames defenseman Dion Phaneuf—and was less than kind. "I just want to comment on how it's become like a common thing in the NHL for guys to fall in love with my sloppy seconds," Avery said tastelessly as the cameras rolled.

For uttering those 26 words, Avery was suspended six games by the NHL, which also penalized him in an unprecedented manner by forcing him into anger management counseling. Bettman described Avery's comments as the latest in "a type of conduct that is repetitive, inappropriate and perhaps antisocial . . . What guided me in this case was we needed to be clear that this was not acceptable and not representative of what our players do . . . I wanted it to be clear to the fans that this is not something we tolerate, particularly fans with children, who may have to explain to them what this statement was."

Consider what Bettman does and doesn't consider antisocial behavior that could harm the delicate eyes and minds of children: checks from behind, slashing, knee-on-knee attacks, and other on-ice acts of lunacy qualify as normal behavior. Callous and rude *words*, on the other hand, are symptoms of unstable and dangerous mindsets that must be stopped at once.

Don't attempt to apply normal rules of logic here. The NHL operates in its own philosophical vacuum, always doing its best to belittle or disregard any intrusion from the outside (real) world.

• • •

That said, don't kid yourself. When the NHL wants to move quickly to address a problem, it can move with whiplash-inducing speed. With the snap of Campbell's fingers, Avery was suspended for six games—ostensibly for doing nothing more than making a fool of himself in Calgary.

Another incident, in which Avery was also involved, further underscores what the league can accomplish and how quickly it can take action when it has the impetus and backbone to stamp out a particular problem. In April 2008, Avery's New York Rangers took on their archrivals, the New Jersey Devils, in New Jersey for a first-round playoff game. During that game, and in a display of relative ingenuity not seen before on an NHL rink, Avery parked himself in front of Devils goalie Martin Brodeur. Facing Brodeur, Avery began waving his stick—at eye level—in Brodeur's face. The following day, Campbell and the NHL sent out a news release announcing that the unsportsmanlike conduct penalty had been reinterpreted to include swinging a stick in a goaltender's face.

The league can call it a reinterpretation all it wants, but in essence, it made up the Sean Avery Rule—instantly—to address behavior it deemed unseemly.

In the summer of 2010, the NHL also moved quickly to eradicate what it perceived as a problem when star right-winger Ilya Kovalchuk attempted to sign a contract with the

New Jersey Devils. The initial contract Kovalchuk signed was worth $102 million and would have kept him with the organization for a staggering 17 years—what would have been a new NHL record for contract longevity. However, NHL officials rejected the contract the following day on the grounds that the deal "circumvented" salary cap regulations (in part, because of the total term of the contract; and in part, because the payout was heavily skewed and front-end loaded so that Kovalchuk would have been paid the league minimum at the end of the deal). More than six weeks later, and after an arbitrator's decision in the league's favor nullified the contract, the Devils and Kovalchuk submitted a restructured deal that came in at 15 years and $100 million. The league accepted the new contract and ostensibly rewrote the collective bargaining agreement on the fly and in its favor. More evidence the league can take action quickly when there's a will.

Easily the saddest example of how quickly the NHL can move when it wants to is the tragedy of a fan death in Columbus in March 2002. Thirteen-year-old Brittanie Cecil was at Nationwide Arena watching the Columbus Blue Jackets play the Calgary Flames, when a puck deflected over the glass and into the stands behind the net, striking her in the head. Though Cecil left the game under her own power and exhibiting no signs of massive trauma, her skull had been fractured by the puck; she died in an Ohio hospital two days later from complications from a torn vertebral artery.

In response to Cecil's death, the NHL implemented mandatory netting at both ends of all its arenas by the start of the following season. The league understood that not to move quickly to protect its paying customers would be to leave itself vulnerable to liability lawsuits and the negative public optics of appearing not to have learned a lesson from an unspeakably awful accident.

So, when it is sufficiently motivated to do so, you see that there's never anything that stops the NHL from moving to halt or address a particular situation. The trouble is, when it comes to its most important employees—the players who show up night after night for 82 games during the regular season and then the playoffs—the league always finds a way to rationalize its much slower response to making the game as safe as possible.

• • •

Take the case of Kurtis Foster, a defenseman who was playing for the Minnesota Wild in 2008. While being chased into his own end by San Jose Sharks forward Torrey Mitchell, Foster was knocked into the end boards and broke his left femur. What made things even worse was that there were complications in the operation to repair Foster's femur, such that he nearly died on the operating table and almost had his leg amputated.

And for what? A run-of-the-mill icing play? It made little sense to many people who expected the NHL to finally address the dangerous icing chase and change the rules to a different system—such as a hybrid icing rule in which the league's linesmen have the discretion to whistle the play dead if a linesman believes the defending player will reach the puck before the player chasing him. (Under this scenario, if the linesman believes the attacking player has a chance to reach the puck first, then the race would be allowed to play out.) That wouldn't have eliminated the risk involved, but only minimized it. Yet even that was too much for NHL officials. The season after Foster's injury, the league did not adopt the hybrid icing rule; instead it passed a rule that said:

> *Any contact between opposing players while pursuing the puck on an icing must be for the sole purpose of playing the puck and not for eliminating the opponent from playing the puck. Unnecessary or dangerous contact could result in penalties being assessed to the offending player.*

In other words, the NHL was prepared to discourage dangerous actions—but only to a certain degree. It was not ready to alter—even slightly—the structure of play to systematically reduce the danger of an icing play. It was prepared to live with more Kurtis Fosters as the cost of doing business.

No wonder Foster spoke out and openly lobbied for more player safety in a TSN interview in 2010. Some people may not comprehend how tough it is for a player to make his voice heard in an NHL community that demands near-total deference to authority; but Foster—who courageously rehabilitated his leg and returned to the league in 2009—spoke up because he didn't want one of his colleagues to suffer a fate similar to or worse than his.

Can you imagine any other game in which an athlete who has overcome a gruesome injury to compete again speaks out and says, "Hey folks, the governing body of my sport isn't doing enough to prevent someone from nearly dying like I did in competition," and that governing body blatantly ignores him and callously carries on?

Can you imagine a warehouse worker narrowly escaping being killed in an industrial accident triggered by a dangerous workplace, and the owner of the warehouse refusing to correct the conditions? That story would make front-page newspaper headlines in any civilized city on the planet.

Within the NHL's city limits, that's par for the course. In the NHL, players are replaceable. The league has historically held the notion that fans pay to see the team, not individual players or their irreplaceable talents. Team owners and their minions believe what veteran agent Allan Walsh was told at the 2010 NHL All-Star Game in Raleigh, N.C., when the topic turned to concussed and sidelined superstar Sidney Crosby:

> An NHL executive said to me, "Everybody's whining because [Crosby] is out, but nobody really cares about this issue. All we'll do is find another player to hype and everybody will forget about Sid." I wonder how much of that attitude permeates through NHL headquarters.

Walsh isn't the only one left wondering. It is only natural to assume NHL team owners are acting primarily in their own best interests as the annals of the NHL are fraught with story after story of NHL owners who treat their players as property and not people—as racehorses to be ridden until their bodies break down.

Virtually every night of every season, players are permitted to cut each other down physically with little to no repercussion to dissuade them from doing the same thing, or worse, next time they're on the ice.

• • •

It truly is hard to know where to begin cataloguing how common over-the-top antics are in the modern-day NHL. We've already covered the madness of Matt Cooke, the insouciance of Sean Avery, the brutality of Todd Bertuzzi, and the callous indifference toward Kurtis Foster's agony and subsequent crusade. Certainly, the casual observer would wonder, there couldn't be other examples as bad or worse than those?

Surely enough, the observer would discover the horrible truth: that vicious acts of potentially enormous bodily harm are the stock-in-trade of an entire class of professional hockey player; that some of those players—some call them enforcers, but I call them Dancing Bears, as they're giant men trained to perform unnatural acts for a crowd's enjoyment—now train in mixed martial arts in the off-season instead of training as hockey players; and that occasional outbursts of stick-swinging, spearing, and using skates as weapons by the league's so-called "policemen" (usually those same Dancing Bears) are masked by the league with the euphemisms of "letting off steam," "keeping the other team in check," and "boys being boys."

Does the "rap sheet" built up by a 15-year NHL veteran named Chris Simon read like that of a boy being a boy? He used a racial epithet against an opponent, cross-checked a member of the opposing team in the throat, and kneed an opponent. And on each of these occasions, Simon was simply slapped on the wrist.

Not a word of that is an exaggeration, nor does it represent the worst of Simon's behavior. He marauded through the Canadian junior hockey system (racking up 439 penalty minutes in 144 Ontario Hockey League games) and, by the time he made it to the NHL in 1993, was an increasingly rare breed—a fearsome, six-foot-three goon who had real and valuable hockey skills; he scored a career-high 29 goals for Washington in 1999–2000 and finished with at least 10 goals in seven seasons.

But as we see with so many so-called policemen of the game, Simon began to unravel toward the end of his NHL days such that his increasingly animalistic acts essentially forced the league to wash its hands of him.

Over a nine-month span in 2007, Simon (at the time, a New York Islander) was suspended a total of 55 games for two separate, repugnant incidents. The first time, he was banned 25 games in March for swinging his stick directly and intentionally into the face of another player; the second time, he was suspended 30 games in December for purposefully stepping down with his skate on an opponent's leg.

Remember, this is someone the hockey establishment wants you to believe makes the game safer. The NHL argues that Simon's ability to throttle an opponent polices other players into playing responsibly. But clearly, "policemen" such as Simon wind up breaking the league's laws as often as any other type of player.

The relative heavy-handedness of the suspensions must have struck like thunderbolts to Simon's psyche. After all, prior to 2007 the longest Simon had been suspended was three games for the racial slur; he was suspended for only one game for the cross-check across the throat; and two games for the kneeing incident.

Before 2007, Simon was suspended on six occasions yet only sat out a total of 10 games. And so the pattern we saw with Bertuzzi emerges again: the NHL and hockey's culture failed to send a no-nonsense message to an overly aggressive player early in his career. When that aggression bubbled over, the game's establishment instantly reclassified him as a pariah.

Simon attempted to blame the stick-swinging incident on what he called a concussion suffered at the hands of Rangers goon Ryan Hollweg, the player at whom Simon swung his stick. Then, the day after he stepped down with his skate on the leg of Penguins agitator Jarkko Ruutu, Simon agreed to take a voluntary leave from the Islanders saying he needed time away from the game.

The league was happy to oblige Simon and handed him the second-longest suspension in history, behind only Marty McSorley's one-year ban in 1999–2000 for his assault on Donald Brashear. Simon came back for one more game with the Islanders and was then traded to Minnesota Wild, where he played the final 10 games of his NHL career. Following that, Simon signed to play in the Russia-based Kontinental Hockey League; in more than 40 games in his first year, he racked up 263 penalties. Apparently, if he'd learned any lessons from his eight previous suspensions, it was that there are only so many times you can run amok in the NHL before you have to take your Dancing Bear act elsewhere.

• • •

In the enforcer community, little has changed since Simon last played an NHL game—both in terms of player attitudes and supplementary discipline. That's illustrated perfectly by examining the trials, tribulations, and psychotic episodes of goon Trevor Gillies, who also happened to be wearing an Islanders jersey when he snapped on the ice twice in 2011.

If you didn't know any better, the story of Gillies would sound inspirational. Here was a career minor-leaguer enjoying his first extended stretch of NHL games at the advanced age of 32. All Gillies' bus rides in the ECHL and American League since turning pro in 1999 were finally paying off with a major-league salary of $500,000.

However, scratch the surface of that story and you'll quickly sniff out the rotten forces responsible for Gillies' ascent to the Islanders roster.

In his first professional season, Gillies amassed 240 penalty minutes (PIMs) in 61 games. In his sophomore year, he "improved" that number—to 303 PIMs in 63 games. The year after that, he had 341 PIMs in 69 games. Unlike Simon, Gillies has no discernible talents other than his ability to maim while keeping his balance on a pair of skates. Since 1999, Gillies has scored eight goals (never more than two in a single season at any level) and 40 points in 619 games as a pro. He does have 2,739 PIMs in those 619 games, though.

Gillies never deserved to wear an NHL jersey at all. He was playing regularly as an Islander in 2010–11 mainly because of the fighting fetish of GM Garth Snow—who enjoyed throwing down his gloves and fighting on a number of occasions as an NHL goalie—and because of a slew of injuries to Isles players possessing actual NHL talent. Indeed, the Isles already had Zenon Konopka—a tough guy who racked up 265 PIMs for the Tampa Bay Lightning in 2009–10—to "stick up" for teammates.

But Gillies was out there anyway, averaging 5.2 shifts and a whopping 2:52 of ice time per game when he wasn't a healthy scratch from the lineup, barely appearing on the official score sheet unless he was drilling his fists into the head of a fellow member of the NHLPA. Even in that small window of playing time, Gillies turned out to be much like Simon and most of the enforcer types in the game: incapable of demonstrating self-discipline while demanding it from players on the other team.

On February 12, 2011, the Islanders were hosting the Pittsburgh Penguins. The game was being contested nine days after the two teams last played in a fight-filled affair highlighted—or, depending on your perspective, "low-lighted"—by a goalie fight that saw Penguins netminder Brent Johnson floor Isles counterpart Rick DiPietro with a single punch that broke several bones in DiPietro's face and sidelined him for weeks.

So much for those arguing that nobody gets injured in a fight. Throughout this book, you'll see many examples proving otherwise.

Naturally, Campbell and the NHL hadn't disciplined anyone involved in the DiPietro/Johnson fight. If they would have done so, they might have calmed the anger of those on both sides who were seeking retribution; but because they did not, when the two teams clashed again nine days later, Gillies became what the North American game's culture had trained him to become: a merciless, manic, heat-seeking missile bent on revenge.

In hockey's twisted "code," Gillies got that revenge—though not by trading punches with Johnson (who had to defend himself against Micheal Haley, yet another goon-type Isles player, in one of many disgraceful moments in the game). Instead, Gillies elbowed Penguins left-winger (and non-goon) Eric Tangradi in the face, punching him several times while Tangradi was down on the ice and taunting him from one of the exit areas to the ice surface.

Gillies wasn't alone in his abject stupidity during that February 11th debacle of a game; in total, 65 penalties were assigned (including 15 fighting majors and 20 misconducts) and 10 players were ejected. But, other than the automatic

10-game suspension Penguins winger Eric Godard received for leaving the bench and joining the fracas, Gillies received the harshest suspension—nine games.

I don't believe that subjecting Gillies to suspension totaling little more than 10 per cent of an 82-game regular season was enough. But for argument's sake, let's say he received a fair suspension, served his time, and deserved a second chance. Want to guess what he did in his first game back after that suspension (when the Isles took on the Minnesota Wild on March 2)?

If you guessed that he played two shifts without incident, but during his third shift, he reacted to seeing a teammate being hit from behind and into the boards by blindsiding another opponent with a targeted elbow and fist to the head, you'd be absolutely right. Gillies played a total of 1:51 against the Wild that night, and when Minnesota agitator Cal Clutterbuck knocked Isles center Justin DiBenedetto into the side boards, Gillies immediately exploded into Clutterbuck with the intent of doing maximum damage to the Wild winger's upper body.

Clutterbuck wasn't seriously injured on the play, but with the NHL's new rule banning blindside headshots regardless of a victim's condition, and with Gillies' newfound notoriety coming out of the Penguins brawl, it would have been easy, understandable, and admirable for the league to suspend him for the Islanders' remaining 17 regular season games and attempt to put other reckless players on notice.

Instead, the NHL suspended Gillies for 10 games—one more than he got for the serious transgression he committed less than a week-and-a-half earlier. And in the future, if he does something as reprehensible as either of his prior incidents, one can only assume, based on the league's last ruling, that he'll be suspended for 11 games next time.

• • •

But it's not only the goons who are responsible for the on-ice incidents that stain the game or deprive it of its precious talents (i.e., the skills and personalities of the players). Sometimes it's the most well-liked players who are in the spotlight for the wrong reasons.

That was true on March 8, 2011, when towering Boston Bruins defenseman Zdeno Chara shoved Montreal Canadiens left-winger Max Pacioretty into an iron stanchion in Montreal's Bell Centre arena. Because the play happened on a puck chase, with both players pushing at full speed, when Chara pushed Pacioretty as he went to move by him and down the ice, Pacioretty's head went directly into the stanchion and, after coming to a halt, he wasn't moving.

The crowd and both benches were hushed instantly, all fearing they might have just witnessed a death on the ice. Luckily, Pacioretty "only" suffered a severe concussion and a fractured vertebra in his neck.

As with every instance of NHL violence, the aggressor (in this case, Chara) said he meant no intentional harm to the victim. And on some level, he should be believed; at six-foot-nine and 225 pounds, Chara is one of the biggest players in league history and could severely injure virtually anyone if he so chose—or even if he didn't mean to, as he repeated often after the Pacioretty incident.

Canadiens fans were angry and genuinely incensed—sure, primarily because this was one of their beloved Habs players who was hurt, but there was a legitimate second aspect to their rage: they were upset with the direction in which the sport was headed and wanted the NHL to address their concerns.

Naturally, the NHL did no such thing. The league announced Chara would face neither a fine nor a suspension and called the incident a "hockey play." To be fair, on virtually every shift and in every game there are similar chases like the one that hurt Pacioretty. But in the past, the league has said a player's injury can be a factor in supplemental discipline—and yet it obviously didn't make a difference here.

And that view, in itself, made even more people angry. Incredibly, Air Canada—a longtime advertiser with the league and a charter airline for a number of NHL teams—sent the NHL an angry letter signed by the airline's director of marketing and communications, Denis Vandal, which read:

> As a strong supporter and sponsor of NHL Hockey in Canada and several U.S. cities, Air Canada is very concerned with the state of hockey today. While we support countless sports, arts and community events, we are having difficulty rationalizing our sponsorship of hockey unless the NHL takes responsibility to protect both the players and the integrity of the game. From a corporate social responsibility standpoint, it is becoming increasingly difficult to associate our brand with sports events which could lead to serious and irresponsible accidents; action must be taken by the NHL before we are encountered with a fatality.
>
> Unless the NHL takes immediate action with serious suspensions to the players in question to curtail these life threatening injuries, Air Canada will withdraw its sponsorship of hockey.

When is the last time you heard any business partner of a professional league openly question the league's safety standards? Yet that's the corner the NHL's carnival of violence had pushed Air Canada into.

Canadiens owner Geoff Molson also spoke out after Chara escaped punishment, writing the league his own strongly worded letter and alerting the NHL to his serious concerns for the sport's future.

> *The news of the NHL decision [on not punishing Chara] was a hard blow for both the players and fans of the Montreal Canadiens. It was one which shook the faith that we, as a community, have in this sport that we hold in such high regard.*
>
> *The Montreal Canadiens organization does not agree with the decision taken yesterday by the National Hockey League . . . [o]ur organization believes that the players' safety in hockey has become a major concern, and that this situation has reached a point of urgency. At risk are some of the greatest professional athletes in the world, our fan base and the health of our sport at all levels. Players' safety in hockey must become the ultimate priority and the situation must be addressed immediately. As a proud father of three hockey players, I want to help create a healthy and safe experience for them, and I certainly never want any family to go through what the Pacioretty's [sic] are experiencing at this moment.*
>
> *We understand and appreciate hockey being a physical sport, but we do not accept any violent behavior that will put the players' health and safety at risk. On this specific issue, I am asking for the support of the 29 other NHL owners, to*

address urgently this safety issue. And I am willing to play
a leadership role in coordinating this group effort.

Within the ownership community, Molson already had a philosophical partner in Penguins owner Mario Lemieux, who was unafraid to speak out, even at the risk of being subjected to Bettman's wrath. (Bettman has survived as NHL commissioner since 1993 in part because he has established a certain iron-fisted approach with owners who stray out of line. He has not been above having the league sue a team—as it did with the New York Rangers over website strategy—and his opinion matters greatly to the NHL's most powerful governors/owners.)

Molson and Lemieux gained another notable member of their outraged owners group in the Ottawa Senators' Eugene Melnyk, who—after the Pacioretty incident—went on a Toronto sports radio station to voice his disgust.

"I've been the lone wolf on this for years," said Melnyk. "These goons trying to decimate elite players . . . [it] happened to us with [Senators star Jason] Spezza . . . now [it] happened to *the* elite player in [Sidney] Crosby . . . it's going to continue unless radical stuff happens." Melnyk envisions an easy solution to the madness: "You hit a guy in the head . . . you're gone," he told The Fan 590. "You don't play hockey anymore . . . [that's the] only way to do it."

Melnyk also was very clear in expressing his feelings about fans who loudly moan whenever the topic of fighting is broached.

"[I] don't care about what anybody says about 'we need some violence,'" Melnyk said. "[G]o to wrestling . . . go to cage fighting . . . don't do it in a hockey game with elite players."

The strong rhetoric used by Air Canada and the three NHL team owners—with Lemieux, as you'll see in a couple paragraphs from now, as angry as anyone—was an undeniable indication that the united front the NHL claims to have among its owners and business partners is anything but. The direction of the league is as debatable inside NHL boardrooms as it in the public sphere.

Although relics such as Boston Bruins owner Jeremy Jacobs and Philadelphia Flyers owner Ed Snider still hold much power in NHL boardrooms, Melnyk, Lemieux, and Molson are the wave of future NHL owners. They appreciate players as emotional as well as business investments and are unwilling to let social codes from a bygone era rob them of those investments. They know that consumers of their product give their hearts and wallets over to NHLers and can be lost as fans/consumers if those players are forced out of the game by injuries that could have been prevented.

• • •

Less than a day after the suspensions for the Pittsburgh/Islanders February 11th gong show of a game were announced, an incensed Mario Lemieux issued an extraordinary statement tearing into the NHL and its feeble disciplinary process.

"What happened Friday night on Long Island wasn't hockey," Lemieux said that Sunday. "It was a travesty. It was painful to watch the game I love turn into a sideshow like that."

(Some heavily criticized Lemieux for employing Matt Cooke on his roster. That is valid to a degree, but bear in mind that: (a) Cooke has other skills, having scored 10 or more goals in nine seasons; and (b) some think it is better to have a dangerous player on your side than looking across at you as a member of the opposition. In any case, Lemieux has warned Cooke that his actions will no longer be tolerated by the organization and the player appears to be down to his last shot with the Penguins.)

As we've seen in this chapter, the NHL game has been governed for decades by a clear and intentional philosophy, one that has made it culturally permissible to let players cannibalize each other's talents and earning abilities as professionals.

In some aspects, the NHL is miles ahead of where it once was in terms of player safety. But overall, it isn't close to where it should be. That's why the list of players sacrificed to the hockey gods by the growing plague of head injuries has grown in number every year. That's why Sidney Crosby's career was threatened when he hadn't yet turned 24 years old. That's why—except for in the most extreme of circumstances—you can commit any act of aggression on an NHL rink and expect to be suspended for no more than five percent of your season.

That's why Mario Lemieux, who played with a grace and determination like few others, can now talk with the same fear and disgust as the ankle-breaking Bobby Clarke did in wondering why players no longer bodycheck simply to separate an opponent from the puck.

It's why Lemieux and Clarke can speak with the same unease as former player and GM Mike Milbury. A longtime advocate of fighting—and a man who, during his playing career, once jumped into the stands of the Boston Garden to fight a fan with a shoe—Milbury spoke out in March 2011, questioning the need for designated fighters and ridiculing the age-old, pro-fighting argument that fisticuffs help the players themselves police the game.

You don't have to play the game in a particular way to know something's amiss.

And, that's why the game needs to change at hockey's highest levels. A different approach is necessary both to protect the elite and irreplaceable talent, and to curb recklessness in the amateur leagues, where normal kids and beer leaguers have to live with the aftermath of irresponsible acts. Fittingly, then, Lemieux reserved his strongest sentiments for the league:

> *The NHL had a chance to send a clear and strong message that those kinds of actions are unacceptable and embarrassing to the sport. It failed. We, as a league, must do a better job of protecting the integrity of the game and the safety of our players. We must make it clear that those kinds of actions will not be tolerated and will be met with meaningful disciplinary action.*
>
> *If the events relating to Friday night reflect the state of the league, I need to rethink whether I want to be a part of it.*

At a time when hockey's bloodlust hovers as a threat to its professional and amateur ranks, who can blame him?

"WE SELL HATE"

2 NORTH AMERICAN HOCKEY'S LONG AND BAFFLINGLY PROUD HISTORY OF VIOLENCE

After finishing the previous chapter, you may be tempted to think the outrageous behavior we're seeing at the highest levels of hockey is a relatively new development, a boil that has just begun to bubble up and fester. In fact, nothing could be further from the truth.

In his capacity as NHL commissioner, Gary Bettman has spun the issue of violence in hockey in favor of the traditionalists. The essence of his argument is that there is an inherent risk NHLers assume on the ice and that the sport cannot function properly without the "pressure release" fighting provides.

"Fighting is a part of our game and it always has been," he told a Toronto crowd of businesspeople in 2009. "But it is a small part of the game that receives a disproportionately large amount of attention, particularly in the media . . . [T]o assert, as some have, that there's a culture of violence is inappropriate and utterly inaccurate."

Mr. Bettman can protest all he wants, but shooting the messenger for pointing out the league's unwillingness to punish repugnant player behavior is hardly inappropriate and most assuredly accurate. We may no longer see two entire teams of players trading punches all over the ice as we did in the 1970s, but that doesn't excuse the league from doing more to curb dangerously aggressive play.

Contrary to what Bettman would have you believe, hate is exactly what the NHL sells, and former NHL chief disciplinarian Colin Campbell admitted to it. Asked about a perceived lack of respect among players, Campbell said, "Players are competitive. We sell hate. Our game sells hate."

But just because Bettman, Campbell, and other members of the hockey establishment paint a pretty picture of hockey violence doesn't mean we have to accept their interpretation. Their words don't make fighting any less unnecessary to the modern game. Indeed, we should be looking at the long history of violence in the NHL and their efforts to sell hate as more of a reason to end that mindset as soon as possible and bring the focus where it ought to have been all along—on the skills the players can show within the NHL rulebook.

That said, Bettman was right about the history of the game (the North American game, that is), about always counting fighting as a part of the game. While the sport has cracked down on some of its more outrageously violent aspects, hockey always has been laissez-faire in policing its athletes. And that includes the NHL since it was founded almost a hundred years ago.

Back in the early part of the 20th century, the almighty dollar overshadowed the game, just as it does now. Safety, sanity, and everything else were distant afterthoughts when the NHL was formed. Thus, without a strong league administration to control player behavior and set reasonable punishment standards for those who would not comply, nobody on the ice—not the players, not the officials, not even the people in the stands paying to watch—was safe from having their health severely compromised.

In 1927, 10 years after the NHL was founded, Billy Coutu—a former captain of the Montreal Canadiens—was the first player banned for life by the league when he assaulted referees Jerry Laflamme and Billy Bell before the game between his Boston Bruins and the Ottawa Senators. He then proceeded to touch off a bench-clearing brawl. The president of the NHL, Frank Calder, expelled Coutu for good—or so it seemed. Two-and-a-half years later, the ban was lifted, but Coutu did not return. Since then, nobody has done enough to earn the same penalty.

Of course, we all know a lack of substantive punishments doesn't mean NHLers have been innocent, rosy-cheeked cherubs since that time. To the contrary: while some of the more barbaric stick-swinging incidents and five-on-five brawls have been legislated out of the league, there has been a consistent, predictable number of unsettling incidents each and every season.

As a result, NHL players today know what they always have known: even the most egregious on-ice acts carry with them relatively nominal punishments. They know so because, for nearly 95 years, hockey has had ugly episodes that cast it in a poor public light, yet the men charged with the good of the sport have stubbornly refused to learn any lesson from those episodes and adapt the game accordingly.

● ● ●

In the league's early history, the most infamous incident was the Eddie Shore/Ace Bailey run-in that took place on December 12, 1933, and changed the lives of both players.

Shore shared a link with Coutu from seven years earlier when both were with the Boston Bruins. The two men brawled viciously—*as members of the same team merely practicing together.* Coutu attacked Shore during practice; the former threw the latter to the ice and head-butted him, taunting Shore mercilessly. Shore wasn't known to run away from a fight, so when Coutu (who was a decade older than him) charged with rage in his eyes, Shore gave as good as he got. In the end, both men paid serious prices: Shore nearly had his ear amputated before finding a doctor who would agree to sew it back on; Coutu was knocked unconscious and sidelined for an extended period. (Afterward, only Coutu was punished—a whopping-for-the-time $50 fine that was eventually repaid to him by the league.)

So Shore's tenacity was well established by the time his and Ace Bailey's lives collided on that unfortunate December night in 1933. By that point an established NHL star, Shore skated into the Maple Leafs right-winger from behind, knocking Bailey into the ice and unconscious, and fracturing his skull.

"I was skating with my head down and I didn't see Bailey until it was too late," said Shore, who died in 1992. "There was no bad feeling between us. It was purely accidental."

Two months after Bailey was hurt, on Valentine's Day of 1934, the NHL staged its first-ever All-Star Game in Toronto, with the financial proceeds pledged to Bailey's rehabilitation. Shore played in the game and brought the sell-out Maple Leaf Gardens crowd to rapturous applause when he shook hands with Bailey (dressed in street clothes) at center ice.

Nevertheless, the incident lived within Shore, haunting him for years afterward. Although Bailey had recovered—and although the days of players wearing helmets was decades away—he had come very close to dying in the immediate two-week period after the incident and never again played hockey. And despite Shore's protestations that the incident was a mere accident, the fact was that when he laid into Bailey he was seeking retribution for an earlier hit in the game that legendary Maple Leaf King Clancy had applied to him.

Perhaps that's why Shore became one of the first NHLers to speak out about the unnecessary and unnerving elements of the game.

In the October 24, 1953, edition of *The Hockey News*, a long-retired Shore had this to say: "Don't you see that one of the drawbacks of our game is that the fine natural ability, the deftness, the dexterity of the better player is deteriorated because of our failures in applying the strict letter interpretation of our rules?"

Shore understood that hockey could be so much more than what the game's gatekeepers allowed it to be. But his cries fell on deaf ears and the players and coaches were left to their own devices. And that's why each and every season the lunatic behavior continued.

Sometimes, the lunacy could be found in the coaching ranks.

On February 8, 1950, Chicago coach and former NHLer Charlie Conacher and his Blackhawks were taking on the Detroit Red Wings, when he suddenly snapped, first grabbing a referee by the sweater, then punching a sportswriter after the game. Unsurprisingly, league president Clarence Campbell levied not a single punishment on Conacher. In speaking about the assault on the sportswriter, Campbell said it was a "personal matter between two men."

That sent the local press into a frenzy. Interestingly, many of their opinions still apply to the game and its problems today.

"A new rule is needed in hockey immediately where Conacher is concerned," wrote *Detroit Times* sports editor

Bob Murphy. "Either Campbell should insist on Conacher taking saliva tests at certain intervals during a game, or newspapermen covering the hockey beat for self-protection should be allowed to equip themselves with brass knuckles or blackjacks."

Detroit News sports editor H.G. Salsinger was even more pointed in his criticism of Campbell and the league:

It is about time that the men who own franchises in the National Hockey League clean up their investment. Professional hockey has gotten completely out of hand. It has become a "muggs" game where muckerism is condoned.

Hockey today is in a position similar to that of baseball at the turn of the century when the language and conduct of players kept the decent element out of the parks . . . what would happen to Conacher if he conducted himself similarly in baseball, football or any of the other professional sports? His time would be extremely brief.

Why does hockey stand for conduct that is not tolerated in any other game? . . . The sooner hockey rids itself of the hoodlum grip and elects a president who will be more than a figurehead, the better off the game will be. In its present state it is deteriorating into an alley brawl and a disgusting one.

Salsinger was right—hockey was allowed to continue to deteriorate. Indeed, the art of intimidation ceased to be only one facet of the game and instead became a driving force for the architects and managers of most teams. And in many regards, player behavior sunk to its nadir—not just in the NHL, but in the upstart World Hockey Association (WHA) as well during the 1975–76 season.

It began on November 5, 1975, when Detroit Red Wings left-winger Dan Maloney attacked Toronto Maple Leafs defenseman Brian Glennie from behind, pummeling him with his stick and fists and knocking Glennie unconscious. This did not sit well with then–Ontario Attorney General (and future CEO of the Canadian Football League) Roy McMurtry, who announced a provincial crackdown on hockey violence and promptly charged Maloney with assault causing bodily harm. The incident was the first to go to full trial, and although he completed enough community service to negate the charge, Maloney wasn't permitted to play in Toronto for two years.

Meanwhile, the WHA, a business in direct competition with the NHL (and one signing away as many elite players from the NHL as it could), had its own share of embarrassments in its brief period of operation. The worst involved Rick Jodzio, an enforcer for the Calgary Cowboys, and Marc Tardif, star left-winger for the Quebec Nordiques, during an April 11 playoff game in Quebec City.

Tardif turned out to be the leading goal scorer in the history of the WHA (with 316 goals in 446 regular-season games) and had the second-most points of any WHAer; before he left the NHL for Quebec, he had been drafted second overall by the Canadiens, won two Stanley Cups with Montreal, and had two straight NHL seasons of at least 25 goals scored.

None of that mattered to Jodzio, who lined up Tardif as he skated along the boards, charged at him, threw himself through the air, and cross-checked him, then peppered him with punches as Tardif lay prone and unconscious on the ice. Both benches emptied immediately, and for the next 20 minutes, an ugly brawl took place between the teams. Quebec police were forced to step onto the benches and the ice to break up the fights between the players. Eleven players were ejected from the game, and the referee levied 179 minutes in penalties.

Tardif was taken off the ice on a stretcher and diagnosed with a serious concussion that left him unable to play for the rest of the playoffs—or at all, for that matter, until training camp the following season.

The outrage over Jodzio's assault on Tardif was instantaneous; minutes after the game ended, the Calgary team received death threats against Jodzio and they had to sneak him out of town before any locals could touch him. The WHA suspended Jodzio for the remainder of the playoffs, but he was back and playing in the league again the following season. However, he didn't get away scot-free. Quebec police charged him with assault, a charge to which he pled guilty and was fined $3,000.

It wasn't that simple for Tardif. When he returned to the ice, he was never the same player; he suffered from dizziness and his offensive totals more or less steadily declined. In a sense, he was one of the first players to exhibit noticeable effects of brain damage, yet even that wasn't enough to force WHA officials to take serious measures to eradicate the needless play that leads players to take the actions that Jodzio took. Four days after the Tardif/Jodzio debacle, the defending Stanley Cup champion Philadelphia Flyers faced off against the Toronto Maple Leafs in Game 3 of their quarterfinal series, with storied Maple Leaf Gardens providing the memorable setting.

Although the Leafs won the April 15 game by a score of 5–4, Toronto benefited from a wildly lopsided 16–3 advantage in power play opportunities. After it was over, the Flyers said referee Dave Newell called the game "too closely," meaning the officials called too many penalties and should've let the players play without interference. But other, less-tilted opinions watched the Broad St. Bully Flyers take numerous liberties with the Leafs—especially (and note the pattern here) Swedish imports Inge Hammarstrom and star defenseman Borje Salming.

Not all the Leafs were against fisticuffs and aggression the way Salming and Hammarstrom were. Toronto's Kurt Walker speared noted enforcer Dave Schultz in the first period of the game, setting off the first brawl of the night.

With the Leafs leading 4–3 in the second period, Don Saleski, another Flyers goon, was assessed a tripping penalty by Newell. When he got into the penalty box, a fan in the stands struck him with some thrown ice cubes—and that made Saleski snap. He whipped around and attempted to confront the fan, but a Toronto police officer grabbed his stick as the crowd around them grew more agitated. Meanwhile, on the ice, Flyers defenseman Joe Watson went to the penalty box area to support Saleski. Watson took his stick and swung it over the Gardens glass, hitting another officer who had come in to help calm the situation. But the calm didn't last long, as Flyers rookie Mel Bridgman quickly drilled Salming with a behind-the-net check, followed by a few punches before Salming could turn to face him.

The game ended in Toronto's favor, but the real contro-versy didn't begin until the next day, when Ontario Attorney General Roy McMurtry announced his intent to file criminal charges against Watson, Bridgman, and Saleski.

Saleski and Watson were charged with common assault, possession of a dangerous weapon, and assaulting a police offi-cer. Bridgman was charged with assault causing bodily harm. All players had to report to the local police station before being fingerprinted and released to play in time for Game 4.

In the next game in Toronto, Flyers goon Dave Schultz was being escorted off the ice after a misconduct penalty when he became involved in an altercation with a Leafs fan. As they did for Bridgman in Game 3, members of the Flyers team rushed over to aid their teammate, and Flyers defenseman Bob Kelly threw one of his gloves into the stands where it struck a female Gardens usher in the face. The following day, McMurtry charged Kelly with assault causing bodily harm.

Rather than recoil in horror that his own employees had been charged with a crime, NHL commissioner Clarence Campbell railed against McMurtry and the Ontario legal system for daring to interfere in what he considered to be the league's business.

"Hockey today is patsy compared to what it was in the days of the six-team NHL," said Campbell, who refused to suspend or even fine the Flyers for their actions and, incredibly, blamed the issue on the power of television and not the acts shown on television. "The increased coverage via TV and the [league's] expansion throughout the United States has placed it more in the spotlight."

However, not everyone at the time saw it as Campbell did. Here's a statement made by a prominent hockey figure after McMurtry laid charges against the Flyers:

Everybody knows where the trouble comes from. [It's] certain players on every team. Any fan can name them.

If management were to tell those guys that a condition of their future employment is bringing an end to all this nonsense, then it would stop. And the way to make management do that is to make this stuff so costly [in terms of fines] no coach could put up with it.

Who said that? None other than then–NHL Players' Association executive director Alan Eagleson.

You could parachute his quote into any discussion about the NHL's behavioral problems today and not a word of it would be out of place or dated. It applied the first day the league hung its shingle, and it applies to Gary Bettman and his tacit acceptance of Matt Cooke and any number of current NHLers.

Yet Eagleson's words obviously carry no weight in the NHL's corridors of power. Indeed, skill-dependent teams such as the 1970s-era Montreal Canadiens and 1980s-era New York Islanders and Edmonton Oilers have proven to be a dying breed in Gary Bettman's NHL, and the notoriously thuggish Philadelphia Flyers of the 1970s have proven to be the template for the hockey we know today.

• • •

All along, some of the greatest players in the history of the NHL have fully understood that hockey and its overall popularity have been restricted by the game's gatekeepers, who unabashedly cater to the base instincts of its athletes.

All-time superstar left-winger Bobby Hull was one of those players. After a Hall-of-Fame career with the Chicago Blackhawks, Hull was playing for the WHA's Winnipeg Jets in October 1975 when he decided to sit out a weekend (including one game and the team's practices) to draw attention to what he called "goon hockey" that was impeding the skills of the team's nine European players. The game was allowing lesser-skilled and more aggressive types to overwhelm skilled European and North American players like Hull and his teammates, and he wasn't going to keep quiet about it as was hockey tradition.

Hull originally intended to sit out far longer, but returned because he didn't want to hurt the team or punish the fans for his beliefs. And Jets management stood by him for his convictions.

"We feel he's a credit to the game and a responsible man who's strong-willed about the game so we respected his wishes to try and do something about it," Jets then-GM Rudy Pilous said of Hull's protest.

A short time later, after the breakout of violence in April 1976, Hull went public and was far more vocal regarding his dissatisfaction with the direction in which hockey was headed. Saying that he was prepared to retire after the 1976 WHA playoffs, Hull's disgust with what hockey had become was unmistakable and he made it clear with reporters:

> I've always said that I'd quit when the game is no longer fun for me. Well, it's not. It's becoming a disaster. The idiot owners, the incompetent coaches, the inept players are dragging the game into the mud. They're destroying it with their senseless violence. The game is no pleasure anymore. It's an ordeal.

Hull was not alone as a superstar NHL athlete who believed the game had gone off the rails.

> I've always been against violence [in hockey], against fighting, legendary Canadiens defenseman, coach and GM Serge Savard told me in 2007. [NHL commissioner Gary] Bettman comes out and says fighting is part of the game. Well, that depends what you want to do with your game. We're the only sport that allows it.

Evidence of Savard's longtime stance against the normalization of fighting in hockey and the promotion of a revenge-oriented game dates back to his playing days, when he was a perennial NHL all-star, Conn Smythe Trophy winner as the most valuable player in the 1969 playoffs, and a key cog in the last true Canadiens dynasty. This is not a man who had a revelation after years of crossing the line from athlete to avenger. This is someone who always saw the game as an art form—not some lowbrow monster truck rally on ice.

In January 1976, Savard and the Canadiens played the Soviet Union's most dominant team, the Moscow-based Red Army Club, as part of a so-called "Super Series" exhibition tournament between the NHL's best teams and a handful of top teams from Russia. The Cold War between North America and communist countries like the USSR was years away from ending, meaning that tensions were running high and every effort was made to paint the Soviet teams as comprised of cold, robot-like players who had the skill, but not the "heart" (hockey code for "resolve"), to win hard-contested games.

But after the Canadiens and Red Army skated to a 3–3 tie, Savard spoke of the Soviets not with contempt, but abject admiration.

"I like the style the Russians play for many reasons," Savard told the Montreal *Gazette* at the time. "I like it because it can't help but improve the skills of a hockey player. For too long we've had to put violence into our game, fighting and hitting guys over the head with your stick because that's what the crowd wanted to see. Or what we thought the crowd wanted to see."

Unlike the 1972 Summit Series won by Canada, in part due to Clarke's stick-swinging sins, the Super Series games were not marred by over-the-top shenanigans. It made Savard wonder what the NHL game would look like—and how many more people might count themselves as hockey fans—if North America took its cues from the Russians.

"Tonight you saw real hockey, and the crowd liked it, didn't they?" Savard said after the tie against the Red Army, before turning his attention to the inferior brand of skilled hockey common to the North American game. "It's impossible to improve our skills the way we're playing the game now. Worse still, there are a lot of potentially great hockey players who never make it to our league because of the emphasis on brutality. Great little guys with all the skills but not the physiques to take the punishment."

Later that same year, Savard's Canadiens faced off against the down-and-dirty Flyers in the Stanley Cup final. In many ways, the series served as a judgment on two very different ways the game could be played. The Flyers were rugged beyond what any NHL team was doing and, entering the series, they had won the Cup for two consecutive seasons.

The Habs, on the other hand, were made from skill and speed. They had Hall-of-Famers Guy Lafleur, Steve Shutt, and Ken Dryden, among many others, who never would perpetrate the on-ice crimes Philly's Bob Clarke did. Montreal was all about the essence of hockey, and the Flyers, while talented enough, were famous for their excessive, unhealthy disregard for the well-being of their opponents.

As it turned out, the Canadiens routed the Flyers, sweeping the series in four games to claim the 19th Cup in franchise history. And Savard spoke openly and passionately afterward about the importance of Montreal's win in the grand scheme of things:

"This is not only a victory for the Canadiens," Savard said after the sweep. "It is a victory for hockey. I hope that this era of intimidation and violence that is hurting [Canada's] national sport is coming to an end. Young people have seen that a team can play electrifying, fascinating hockey while still behaving like gentlemen."

In his post-playing-career days as an NHL executive, Savard tried his best to effect positive change in the way the game was contested. But up against a corporate juggernaut and a league ownership power core that liked the chaos just the way it was, he was unable to push hockey closer to modernity.

Like many, Savard compares those who say fighting is necessary to the game to those who said obstruction—hooking and holding, clutching and grabbing, effectively inhibiting skill—was also essential.

"When I met Bettman [after the 2004-05 lockout], I told him, 'Remember what I said in the [NHL board of] directors' meetings years ago when you asked if there was anything wrong with the game and nobody said a word?'" says Savard, who, like many of us, isn't against a spontaneous fight, but is adamant the sport's goons [the "designated hitters", as he said] must go. "I said, 'Yeah, there's something wrong with the game—there's hooking and grabbing,' and it took [the league] years to get rid of it."

● ● ●

Another NHL Hall-of-Famer well known for his preference of skilled hockey is New York Islanders superstar right-winger Mike Bossy.

Like Savard, the four-time Stanley Cup champion and holder of multiple league records had the proper vision of the game from his earliest days. He wasn't one of those players who'd been converted to his current views after being victimized by hockey's culture of violence. Instead, Bossy always knew what hockey could be—and that the North American game's obsession with violence and physical decimation always restricted it from realizing its full potential as a sport.

"Saying that I have to accept [what hockey is today] is difficult, since I never accepted it or approved of it when I played," Bossy told me in 2011. "It's tough—I don't like it. It's been part of the game for so long, it's something that doesn't want to go away. I keep on hoping that with more and more severe suspensions, that the people who are excessive about it will be reduced in the long term."

Bossy, who scored 50 or more goals in the first nine of his 10 NHL seasons—a record not even Wayne Gretzky could equal or break—was constantly battered and bruised by less-talented players. But he never bought into the idea that his bruises gave him full license to attack players as he'd been attacked. When he stopped playing, he had only 210 career penalty minutes; only twice was he whistled for a 10-minute-or-greater penalty, and he never had more than 38 PIMs in a single year.

Such stellar behavior made Bossy an easy choice for the Lady Byng Trophy as the league's most gentlemanly player. It also earned him an unfair reputation as a whiner and a soft player, but all Bossy ever did was play through the constant abuse and excel anyway. Over his relatively short career, Bossy developed a bad back, which forced him into retirement, leading to the reasonable conclusion that yet another spectacular NHL player (in this case, one of the greatest pure offensive talents to ever strap on skates) had his contribution period curtailed by wanton idiocy and hyper-aggressiveness. And still, that wasn't enough of an impetus to get the game's power brokers to reconsider their stance.

Whether or not he was bitter, you couldn't blame Bossy for feeling let down by his sport. In 2001, Bossy told the Hockey Hall of Fame website that he remained displeased with the state of the modern game.

"Fighting is probably less accepted today than in my day," he said. "The days of the goon going out to goad the star player into a fight are over, but that kind of violence has been replaced by checking from behind and stickwork, which are worse than fighting. Players today think nothing of firing an opponent into the boards from behind."

Now in his mid-fifties and an Islanders business executive, Bossy isn't as publicly vocal about his distaste for goon hockey as he once was. In a way, it's hard to blame him: as he noted, it is clear a majority of the hockey establishment wants fighting and cartoon violence to remain in the game—so railing about the illogic of it must feel like tilting at windmills at this stage of his life.

Still, that core belief that hockey can be played without destroying your opponent hasn't gone away. And that noble determination to play the game the right way is a choice Bossy stands behind today.

"When you are one of the better players on the ice, you get all sorts of attention," Bossy said. "Sometimes it's nice, and sometimes it's not so nice. The only way to handle it was to say, 'You know what? You can spear me, you can hook me, you can knock me down, but I'm going to get up and try and perform to the best of my abilities.' That's the way I always looked at it."

• • •

Although this chapter has focused on hockey violence in the near-century the NHL and pro North American hockey leagues have been in existence, you'd require an entire encyclopedia to fully catalog all the inexcusable behavior that has taken place.

We haven't mentioned infamous figures such as all-time frightening behemoth Link Gaetz, ominously nicknamed "The Missing Link" and notorious for amassing 412 penalty minutes in just 65 career NHL games. We haven't mentioned how sad it was to see Gaetz return to the ice in his late thirties to take part in a carnival-sideshow-like, pay-per-view hockey fighter's event, evoking comparisons to a pathetic professional wrestler eking out a meager existence performing in high school gyms for a relative pittance.

We haven't mentioned that, in March 1950, Gordie Howe's incomparable hockey career nearly ended four years after it began when he charged toward Maple Leafs forward Ted "Teeder" Kennedy in a playoff game between Detroit and Toronto. Unfortunately for Howe, Kennedy moved at the last moment and Howe crashed head-first into the boards, fracturing his skull and leading to an operation to alleviate pressure on his brain. Of course, Howe went on to play for decades, but the game once again dodged a significant bullet only by sheer chance and not design.

We haven't mentioned (although we will in a later chapter) Dino Ciccarelli being charged with assault in Toronto for swinging his stick at and connecting with the head of Leafs defenseman Luke Richardson during a 1988 game.

And we haven't mentioned Washington Capitals agitator Dale Hunter nearly crippling New York Islanders star center Pierre Turgeon in 1993, when Turgeon scored a playoff-series-winning goal, only to be drilled into the boards by Hunter. (Turgeon separated his shoulder and Hunter got a 21-game suspension, in part due to the large public outcry.)

We could go on and on. But to say there never has been a shortage of North American hockey players putting each other's lives at risk is a massive understatement.

Has anyone heard so much as a fraction of such untoward behavior reported in Russia, Sweden, Finland, or any other hockey-playing country outside of Canada or the United States? To ask the question is to answer it. It is a phenomenon specific to one continent, one knowingly and carefully interwoven into the fabric of an otherwise thrilling sport.

• • •

When Campbell talked about the league selling hate, he surely didn't intend to convey that fans wind up hating opposing players for otherwise criminal behavior, and surely didn't intend it to mean that the fans also would grow to loathe him, his supplementary discipline office, and the league brass in general for abdicating their duties as the primary protectors of the players.

But both those things are undoubtedly true today. The league sells hate in many ways. How many officials from other sports leagues would dare to argue they sell hate and not an entertaining sports experience? None that I've been able to locate.

As we've seen with recently concussed Sidney Crosby and numerous other stars from one end of the NHL's talent spectrum to the other, the plague of violence embraced by the league doesn't discriminate based on status or any other descriptor. It impacts all players of the game.

And as you'll see in the next chapter, violence in hockey is a plague that has exacted a terrible price from those blessed enough by genetics and hard work to play the game.

SCAR TISSUE

WHAT HOCKEY ALREADY HAS LOST THANKS TO FIGHTING, CONCUSSIONS, AND VANITY

When many in the hockey world began sounding alarms over the rash of head injuries in the 2010–11 season—more than 10 percent of NHL players were diagnosed with a concussion that season—Maple Leafs GM Brian Burke told reporters that, in his opinion, a molehill was being made into a mountain strictly because the league's marquee player was dealing with the problem.

"Frankly, I think the biggest reason we're focused on concussions is because of [Penguins superstar] Sidney [Crosby]," Burke said after the NHL's board of governors meeting at the 2011 All-Star Game in Raleigh, N.C. "If [Leafs journeyman forward] Mike Brown got that concussion, would you [reporters] all be around with cameras asking about concussions? I don't think so."

Therein, folks, lies one of the biggest problems in hockey today—the notion that concussions are an issue solely because of some high-profile victims. Associated with this notion is the often-heard cry of GMs in recent years that the concussion problem is new, that it requires further study before taking action that could affect "the fabric of the game."

Nothing could be further from the truth. It's bad enough baselessly implying that people would not be paying this much attention to concussions if it were a syndrome that only affected fourth-line worker bees or spare defensemen. But to suggest the NHL has been losing players for only a short span of time is outrageous.

In the last decade, head injuries have robbed hockey's greatest league of players of all calibers, at vastly different points in their individual careers. Not all these players were cut down by injuries that could have been prevented, but only by looking at the total carnage can we put to rest Burke's suggestion this is a new and trendy topic soon to recede into the back of the public's mind.

Consider:

- One of the earliest reported concussion victims was former winger Michel Goulet, arguably the greatest player ever to wear a Quebec Nordiques uniform. Goulet scored 40 or more goals in seven of his 15 NHL seasons—including four straight seasons of at least 53 goals per year—and averaged more than a point per game (1,152 points in 1,089 career regular-season games) before he was inducted into the Hockey Hall of Fame in 1998.

  His career ended suddenly at age 33 when, as a member of the Chicago Blackhawks, he fell into the end boards at the famous old Montreal Forum arena during a March 16, 1994, game and was diagnosed with a severe concussion. Goulet continued to suffer post-concussion symptoms more than a decade after he was first injured.

- Brian Bradley was considered the first star player the Tampa Bay Lightning team had after coming into the NHL as an expansion team in 1992. Acquired from Toronto, for whom he had just 10 goals in 59 games in 1991–92, Bradley had a career year in 1992–93, potting 42 goals and 86 points in 80 games.

  Listed generously at five-foot-ten, Bradley never again reached those plateaus (although he did amass 56 assists for Tampa in 1995–96), and after a concussion suffered during a game in Los Angeles in November 1997, doctors told him to stop playing. Thirty-three years old at the time of his retirement after 11 NHL seasons, Bradley continued suffering post-concussion symptoms for two more years.

- In late 1998, two-time Stanley Cup champion Jeff Beukeboom was sucker-punched by Kings goon Matt Johnson and concussed; 33 years old at the time and no shrinking violet himself, Beukeboom missed a handful of games, but returned to play. Two months later, on a relatively harmless collision, Beukeboom suffered another head injury. That was the end for him; he had headaches, memory loss, nausea, and mental fogginess that did not dissipate for months; and he continued to deal with post-concussion symptoms for nearly two years.

- Brett Lindros, younger brother of superstar Eric Lindros, played just 51 career NHL games before head injuries derailed his hockey career for good. The ninth overall pick of the New York Islanders in 1994, Lindros had not yet turned 21 years old and was in his sophomore season when concussions pushed him out of the sport after the 1995–96 campaign.

- One of the most hyped hockey prodigies in the history of the game, former captain of the Philadelphia Flyers—and for a span of nine years, one of the NHL's premier power forwards—Eric Lindros never appeared to be the same player after New Jersey Devils defensive menace Scott Stevens hit him with a devastating body check during a 2000 playoff game. But his problems with concussions began well in advance of that incident.

On many fronts, the elder Lindros is of particular relevance in connection to head injuries and the NHL's self-sacrificial, macho culture. Although he played a take-no-prisoners style, Lindros never appeared to be a perfect fit with the Flyers, his first pro team, the franchise with which he spent eight of his 13 years in the league, and the organizational epitome of the ultra-physical brand of hockey some believe contributed to shortening Lindros' career. At one point in his Philadelphia stint, Lindros had a near total-breakdown in his relationship with ownership and management—particularly then-GM Bob Clarke who, as the years went on, made broad public hints suggesting Lindros was not as tough a player as he could be.

Lindros' first known concussion took place in 1998, resulting in an 18-game absence from Philadelphia's lineup. In 1999, he and the Flyers were in Nashville playing the Predators when he suffered what first was diagnosed as a rib injury. After the game, his teammate and hotel roommate Keith Jones found him "pale and gasping" in a bathtub and was concerned enough to alert team trainer John Worley. When Worley relayed Lindros' condition to team orthopedic specialist Arthur Bartolozzi, he was instructed to send Lindros back to Philadelphia on a commercial airline flight along with injured teammate Mark Recchi. In part thanks to Jones' vehement protestations, Worley refused and insisted Lindros receive immediate medical treatment.

Still, it took three full hours after Jones spoke to Worley before Lindros was admitted to Nashville's Baptist Hospital; by the time he arrived at the emergency ward, "Eric's critical condition was obvious," according to his father and agent, Carl Lindros.

"[Eric] was in shock, sweating, skin color as white as a sheet," Carl Lindros wrote in a 1999 letter to Flyers owner Ed Snider. "[His] resting pulse was almost twice its normal rate."

Lindros was immediately taken into surgery and diagnosed with a collapsed lung resulting from internal bleeding of his chest wall. He had emergency surgery in time and would go on to make a full recovery, but he and his family were incensed at what they perceived as a needless near-death experience narrowly averted only because of a stubborn teammate's refusal to follow team orders.

"We have been advised that had Eric attempted to fly back to Philadelphia as directed by Mr. Worley and Mr. Clarke, Eric would likely have died during or as a result of the flight," Carl Lindros wrote.

Later in the 1999–2000 season, the team stripped Lindros of his captaincy after he again questioned Worley's actions in Nashville. Lindros also sustained two more concussions that season, the latter of which sidelined him through the final 14 games of the regular season and the first two rounds of the 2000 playoffs; he then returned to play for the Flyers in the final two games of their Eastern Conference Final series against New Jersey.

Again, all this happened *before* the Scott Stevens hit.

So when Lindros had his head down, was skating with the puck through the neutral zone in Game 7 of that series and the six-foot-two, block-of-granite Stevens came across the ice to deliver the incredible blow, it was as if Lindros had hit a solid brick wall as he suffered the fifth concussion of his career at the tender age of 27. He was instantly rendered unconscious and never played another second in a Flyers uniform, signing as an unrestricted free agent with the New York Rangers the next season.

Lindros suffered eight concussions in total, and after his first season as a Ranger, the quality of his play dropped off considerably. No longer could he bang bodies as he once did, and his offensive totals dropped in all but one of his final four injury-plagued seasons before he retired following the 2006–07 season. He is still a candidate for entry into the Hockey Hall of Fame, but many lament what might have been if Lindros played a different style, or had alternative doctors who examined and treated him regularly.

- Another victim of Scott Stevens—who, ironically enough, had his own career ended by a concussion in 2004—was Paul Kariya, a superstar in the 1990s for the Anaheim Ducks and easily the greatest-ever NHLer with a Japanese background.

But, like Eric Lindros, Kariya had problems with head injuries long before he was manhandled by Stevens. On February 1, 1998, he was cross-checked in the head by veteran defenseman Gary Suter, derailing Kariya's plans to play for Canada at the Nagano 1998 Olympic Winter Games.

The three-time NHL First Team all-star maintained a prodigious scoring pace after that (although he never again reached the 50-goal mark as he did in the 1995–96 campaign), right up until his Anaheim Mighty Ducks had reached the Stanley Cup final in 2003. In Game 6 of that series, Kariya had just finished making a pass when Stevens lit into him with everything he had. Connecting with his shoulder to Kariya's head, Stevens knocked the then-29-year old into unconsciousness; after a brief trip to the dressing room for further "examination," Kariya returned to the game and scored Anaheim's fourth goal in an eventual 5–2 win.

Kariya was hailed as a hero for shaking off a punishing hit, but in the years after that, his production dropped— from 31 goals with Nashville in 2005–06 to 24 goals with the same team the following season, to 16 goals with St. Louis in 2007–08—and he sat out the entire 2011–11 season with post-concussion symptoms before announcing his retirement in June 2011.

Immediately after making the announcement, Kariya— one of the least accessible, least controversial NHLers I've ever encountered—blasted the NHL's approach to player safety in an interview with Eric Duhatschek of the *Globe and Mail*. He too knows the potential for catastrophe you accept as an elite player. But he also pointed out the league's unwillingness to suspend players, coaches, and owners to a meaningful degree as an example of the reticence the hockey establishment has demonstrated in legitimately cleaning up the game.

"If you want to get rid of it, I'm a believer that you don't go after the employees, you go after the employers," Kariya told Duhatschek. "The first concussion I had, on a brutal, blindside hit, the guy got a two-game suspension. That was in 1996. The last one, from [Buffalo Sabres agitator Patrick] Kaleta, was exactly the same play, and he doesn't get anything. If you start at 10-game suspensions and go to 20, that sends a message to the players. But if you start fining the owners and suspending the coach, then it's out of the game."

The NHL still allows the types of hits that shortened Kariya's career. And despite the league's protestations it is doing all it can, that the game will always carry with it an increased degree of danger, Kariya knows in his heart that there could be dark days ahead if hockey continues on its present course.

"The thing that I worry about is that you'll get a guy who is playing with a concussion, and he gets hit, and he dies at centre ice," Kariya said. "Can you imagine what would happen to the league if a guy dies at centre ice?"

- David Tanabe, like the Lindros brothers, was thought to have a stellar future ahead of him; he was the first graduate of the U.S. National Team Development Program to be selected in the first round of the NHL draft and the team that selected him (the Carolina Hurricanes) was thrilled to add a young defenseman of his caliber to its organization. But in his first season with Carolina, Tanabe suffered a concussion and missed three weeks recovering. Over the next seven years he bounced around the league and never realized his projected potential, retiring in 2008 after receiving another concussion in a game at Toronto's Air Canada Centre.

- Veteran enforcer Stu Grimson, a wholly decent man who went on to work in a prominent role as an attorney with the NHL Players' Association, had one of the greatest nicknames in NHL history—"The Grim Reaper"—because he was a six-foot-five colossus who could throw punches with the best of them. Grimson fought more than 200 times in his 13-year NHL career, had reconstructive surgery on his cheek early in his career, and suffered a slew of head injuries and post-concussion symptoms that piled on one another and eventually forced him to leave the game for good after a December 2000 fight with Georges Laraque.

- Nick Kypreos has turned into one of hockey's better broadcasters and news-breakers, but as an NHL player, he might be best remembered for being part of one of the most brutal and violent hockey fights ever to be televised. During a fight that took place in the 1997–98 pre-season, Kypreos (then playing for the Toronto Maple Leafs) was hit so hard by New York Rangers enforcer Ryan Vandenbussche, he was out cold before his head smacked, face-first, against the ice. Kypreos, 31 at the time, was diagnosed with a severe concussion and retired immediately afterwards.

- Another all-time great, NHL Hall-of-Famer Pat LaFontaine, also had to retire far too soon thanks to a steady stream of head injuries. LaFontaine, who spent his entire pro career playing in New York State, stands out as arguably the greatest American NHLer in history; in nine of his 15 seasons, he scored at least 30 goals, and his 148-point season with the Buffalo Sabres in 1992–93 remains the best offensive total ever recorded by a U.S.-born player. Two years prior to that feat, LaFontaine suffered the first concussion of his career when New York Rangers defenseman James Patrick leveled him with a borderline hit to the head during a 1990 play-off game. LaFontaine (at the time a New York Islander) was knocked out by the hit and failed to regain consciousness on the ice before being removed by stretcher.

"[T]he only thing I can remember was that the trainer was trying to—coming in and out of consciousness, I guess I was starting to swallow my tongue and I was going through a little bit of convulsions," LaFontaine later told the website www.brainline.org. "That was my first real severe concussion which is a grade three and I was sitting in the medical room with the doctors and I was in and out—two or three times and I remember saying at one point to the doctor, 'I'm fine. I'm ready to go. Everything's fine Doc. Put me out there.' And [the doctor] said [the] game's been over for five minutes. I said, 'oh.'"

LaFontaine recovered from that scary experience and brought his game back to superstar level for the better part of the next six seasons. But early in the 1996–97 campaign, he suffered a head injury at the hands of six-foot-six goon Francois Leroux, one that was serious enough for Sabres team doctors and management to refuse to clear him for a return to action in spite of LaFontaine's adamant determination to play again.

LaFontaine did not play again for the Sabres, but was traded to the Rangers in late September 1997. That year, he had 23 goals in 67 games, good enough to tie him for the Rangers' scoring lead. Unfortunately, during a March 16, 1998, game against the Ottawa Senators, LaFontaine accidentally skated into teammate Mike Keane and suffered another concussion, knocking LaFontaine out for the remainder of that season and effectively ending his hockey career at age 33.

- Keith Primeau was a big, burly, often-snarly center who thought nothing of bowling over opponents with his six-foot-five, 235-pound frame. The third overall pick in the 1990 entry draft, Primeau captained both the Carolina Hurricanes and Philadelphia Flyers, played in two all-star games and represented Canada at the 1998 Olympic Winter Games in Nagano, Japan. In his 15 years in the NHL, Primeau had 619 points in 909 regular-season games. But in the ninth game of the 2005–06 campaign, he was rocked by a hit from Montreal's Alexander Perezhogin; it was the last in a long line of concussions he'd suffered and he retired in September 2006, never playing another game. On the subject of concussions, Primeau is now one of the league's more outspoken former players.

- Adam Deadmarsh wasn't an A-level star, but rather a solid B who was a member of Colorado's Stanley Cup championship team in 1995–96 and who won a gold medal with the U.S. Olympic men's team in 1998 at the Nagano Games, and a silver at the 2002 Olympic Winter Games in Salt Lake City, Utah. Deadmarsh was a consistent, two-way threat of a player who scored at least 20 goals in four of his nine NHL seasons. A pair of concussions limited him to just 20 games in the 2002–03 campaign, and he sat out the entire 2003–04 season dealing with post-concussion symptoms. Following the lockout year of 2004–05, Deadmarsh announced his retirement. He was only 30 at the time.

- In the last two seasons alone, more names have been added to the list nobody wants to appear on. Marc Savard was on the verge of helping Boston to contend for its first Cup in nearly four decades when Pittsburgh's Matt Cooke knocked him senseless in the spring of 2010; Savard has yet to fully recover and his career was in jeopardy as this book went to press. Elsewhere, Canucks defenseman Dan Hamhuis suffered his fourth concussion late in the 2010–11 season; young Blues star winger David Perron missed all but 10 games of that same season with post-concussion symptoms; and of course, Penguins superstar Sidney Crosby sat out most of the second half of 2010–11 with the same problem.

In fact, more than 80 NHLers reported suffering a concussion in 2010–11. And those are just the reported ones. Don't forget, many concussions go unreported—intentionally, or because the player will hide symptoms to stay in the lineup.

But it's not always the incidents of fighting and concussions that reveal the NHL's cavalier attitude toward player safety. The NHL also has a lingering, serious problem with eye injuries, yet never has made a priority of protecting players from their own competitive natures. Because of that reticence, unfortunate players and their teams wind up paying dearly.

• • •

The Vancouver Canucks have never won a Stanley Cup in their 40-year history, but looked primed to challenge for a championship in 2011 and got to Game 7 of the Cup final before losing to Boston; one of the main reasons for their confidence heading toward the post-season was the play of center Manny Malhotra, a once highly touted prospect who settled into a role as a defensive and faceoff specialist and signed with the Canucks in the summer of 2010.

Malhotra's season appeared to have ended instantly on the night of March 16, 2011, when a puck struck him directly in the left eye during a game, creating enough damage to jeopardize his career and the sight in the eye. However, thanks to immediate medical attention and the world's top eye doctors, he miraculously returned to play in the Canucks' final six games of the playoffs (albeit, in a limited capacity.)

Despite his return, Malhotra obviously suffered a trauma he wouldn't wish on his worst enemy. But at the risk of appearing callous, Malhotra's Canucks teammates, the team's employees, owners, and its fans all lost out—albeit to a far lesser degree than the 29-year-old. Because Malhotra chose to leave himself vulnerable, because of a perceived competitive advantage that existed only in his head, Vancouver's odds of running the table in the playoffs dropped precipitously, and he could pay for it for the rest of his life.

The people who shout loudest in the NHL's ongoing visor debate are the libertarians. "It should be the players' choice," they say. "How dare you tell professionals how to do their jobs!"

Unfortunately, those folks don't realize that most, if not all, NHLers today grew up wearing a visor and were drafted into the league based on their play wearing basic eye protection. Visors are mandatory in all three major junior hockey leagues in Canada, as well as junior hockey systems in Europe. And in the other main pipeline to hockey's top league, the U.S. college hockey system, a visor isn't enough; NCAA players must wear full facial protection during their games.

But once they reach the NHL, players are told it's acceptable to take a screwdriver to their helmet, remove the protective shield and hit the ice without a visor. After that, it's difficult to understate how good it feels to play without one. The fresh air is right there in their faces; there is no need for the constant, tedious necessity of wiping the steam and sweat from their shields; and there may be a fractional difference in their peripheral vision. So when a fellow player takes a puck or stick in the eye and is significantly affected, players will always find ways to rationalize continuing to play without a visor. They do the same thing when they see their colleagues affected by concussions.

"My fear is the player who sees [another player hurt] and says to himself, 'I feel bad for that guy, but that's not me, that's not going to be me,'" said Keith Primeau. "Believe me, I was the same way when I played."

So they don't learn. And that's why, before Malhotra, there was Bryan Berard, a onetime prospect projected as a superstar-type defenseman adept at creating offense as well as playing solidly in his defensive zone.

In the 1999–2000 season, Berard—the first pick in the 1995 NHL entry draft and the league's rookie-of-the-year in 1996–97—was still in the process of blossoming into a superstar role. As a member of the Toronto Maple Leafs, Berard was in Ottawa in March 2000 taking on the Senators when the stick of Sens winger Marian Hossa cut him across his right eye. Immediately, Berard and everyone in the rink knew the injury was quite serious. Blood poured from the eyeball, which had suffered a detached retina and retinal tear. Doctors at the hospital in Ottawa solemnly told him he might lose the eye altogether; at the very least, his NHL career was in serious jeopardy.

At first, Berard's injury appeared to have ended his playing days; he accepted a $6.5 million insurance settlement soon afterward and did not play during the 2000–01 season. But, determined to play again, he also put himself through seven grueling eye operations during his time on the sidelines and returned to the league for the 2001–02 season with the New York Rangers (and with vision in his injured eye at the league minimum 20/400 level only because of a specially-fitted contact lens).

Although his return was heroic, the injury Berard suffered was a major reason why he never came close to realizing his potential. In the six NHL seasons he played after Hossa's stick injured him, he played for five different teams, never playing for more than one full season in any market.

In early 2011, Berard (who retired in 2009 after spending his last pro season in the Kontinental League) was still of two minds regarding the visor issue. On the one hand, he was fully cognizant of the value of a visor; at the same time, he believes mandating their use would make players more reckless in their play.

"I think [mandating visors] would lead to other problems, because guys will feel more protected," Berard said. "When you have that visor on, it's easier to hit other guys, because you're not worried about breaking your nose or your face getting hit. But it's tough, because I don't want to see guys have to deal with any eye injuries. They're not fun to deal with. And to be honest, once I did put my visor on, it saved me numerous times from cuts, stitches, sticks or pucks deflected up. It definitely protects you, no question."

The gruesome scene in Ottawa scared Berard's Leafs visor-averse teammates into putting one on. But after awhile, they regressed and convinced themselves that protecting their eyes was more of an impediment to their NHL careers than it was a way to extend and protect it.

"I saw some guys try," Berard said. "I saw [Leafs captain] Mats [Sundin] and [defenseman Tomas] Kaberle try to put visors on. They couldn't get used to it, and they saw my injury firsthand. It's something where some guys can get comfortable with one and some guys just can't."

When he returned from the injury, Berard really had no choice but to wear a visor. He made the adjustment with little difficulty and said the "cons" in the pros/cons visor debate essentially arise from a lack of convenience.

"It's more of just a pain in the ass," Berard said of convert-ing to a visor. "After every shift, you get the trainer to wipe them down, or clean them up. It's kind of a nuisance."

Berard is honest enough to admit that, had his eye not been hurt, he likely still would be skating with nothing cov-ering his eyes. But he makes no bones (orbital or otherwise) about the necessity of wearing a visor after that March 2000 game.

"If I didn't get injured, I probably never would've put the visor on," he said. "I was more comfortable without it, but I wanted to protect the one good eye I had left."

Long before Berard was injured, hockey had many chances to learn from its past and reduce the degree of risk to its players. But nobody in a position of power wanted to learn that lesson. The status quo was reinforced, and nobody really noticed—or much cared.

Before Berard, there was Henry Boucha, selected 16th overall by the Red Wings in the 1971 Amateur Draft; Boucha didn't wear a helmet, let alone a visor. Instead, he was known for a trademark headband, and a savvy on-ice style that pro-duced 14 goals and 28 points in his first full season with Detroit, and 19 goals in the following campaign. The Wings traded Boucha to the Minnesota North Stars in 1974, and he had 15 goals in 51 games for his new team. But in a game against Boston, Boucha was involved in a stick-swinging incident with Bruins left-winger Dave Forbes; in the melee, Boucha suffered blurred vision and a cracked bone around his eye, which the State of Minnesota later used as evidence to try and convict Forbes of assault.

Traumatized by the incident, Boucha left the NHL to play for the Minnesota Fighting Saints of the World Hockey

Association the following season, but returned toward the end of the year to play for the Kansas City Scouts. Nine games into the 1976–77 season, Boucha retired from active play at age 25. He was inducted into the United States Hockey Hall of Fame 19 years later.

• • •

Sadly, there are many more eye injury stories where those came from. There are countless examples, as a matter of fact, of players who say all the time that pro hockey is a business, yet who refuse to look at their eyeballs as a necessary tool they require to conduct their business.

When Hall-of-Fame defenseman Al MacInnis was clipped by a high stick from San Jose defenseman Scott Hannan in January 2001, he suffered blurred vision, a bruised cornea, and intense pain behind the eye. Shortly thereafter, MacInnis told the Calgary *Sun* how horrific his experience was.

"The scariest part was when I was coming off the ice, when you know it's the eye," MacInnis said at the time. "You just have that bad feeling. You try to look out, and there is lots of blood and you can't see anything."

MacInnis recovered from his initial eye scare—although he now had a permanent blind spot and had to wear a custom-made corrective lens—but fell victim to a career-ending eye injury less than three years later. Three games into the 2003–04 season during a match against the Nashville Predators, MacInnis began experiencing vision problems that were eventually diagnosed as a detached retina in the same eye Hannan's stick had injured. MacInnis never played another game.

Then there was Anders Hedberg, one of the first and best European-born players to make the jump to the NHL. In January 1985, he had his left retina damaged by an errant stick. Less than three months after Hedberg was hurt by a stick to the eye, so too was Pierre Mondou, a two-time Stanley Cup–winning forward with the Montreal Canadiens; the three-time, 30-goal-scorer retired immediately at age 29. There have been many other pro hockey players who've had serious eye injuries that have left them permanently affected. While names such as Hector Marini, Jamie Hislop, Jeff Libby, Glen Sharpley, and Mark Deyell are hardly common—even to hard-core puck fans—their early retirements from the sport collectively signal a problem that needs urgent attention.

It shouldn't take another victim to make the hockey world realize it must do a better job of guarding its idols. The game has lost more than enough talent as it is.

And given Canada's quickly shifting demographics, the game could be losing even more. As *The Hockey News'* senior writer Ken Campbell detailed in the December 2010 edition, Hockey Canada has analyzed Canadian immigration and birth rates and expects the number of children aged 10–14 will drop by more than 300,000 (from the 2.1 million recorded in 2006) by 2016; if the present-day 9.5 percent participation rate for children in hockey stays the same, the amateur ranks could see as many as 30,000 fewer kids playing and loving the sport.

"When you really start to look at the data, there are some scary things there," Hockey Canada president Bob Nicholson admitted to Campbell. "It's not a crisis today, but if we sit here and do nothing, it's going to be a major crisis."

"I tell [Nicholson], 'I don't want to get overly dramatic, but I get scared because we're going to get whacked here,'" Hockey Canada director of operations Jonah McEachern told Campbell. "We don't want to wake up 20 years from now saying, 'Gee, why do we only have 400,000 kids playing?'"

If there is clear potential of a major crisis threatening to fracture hockey, why would the sport wish to compound it by scaring away children and families bewildered by the North American game's aggression fetish? Hockey needs every kid it can get interested in the game and every family that can afford to invest time, money, and emotion in the grassroots level of the sport. But the game's overseers have yet to embrace that reality, preferring instead to live in their own comfortable bubble.

• • •

Without a doubt, part of the blame for the travesty of player safety and its many wide-ranging ramifications must be directed at the NHL and its team owners. After all, would an art investor who pays millions for a painting have it protected by a narcoleptic security guard? Would a vintage car collector leave his most-prized vehicles alone and running with the keys in the ignition? Never.

Of course, any businessman will do the utmost to protect his investment. Any businessman outside the NHL, that is. In their rush to make money off of players, NHL team owners have paid too much deference to players (in allowing them to dictate the way the game is administrated) and have not insisted on equipment and rules that would create better odds of keeping them injury-free.

Either that, or they truly believe, as some say they do, that the expendability of NHL players makes their safety less of a priority.

That said, the NHL Players' Association cannot escape a share of the blame for the eye injuries players consistently suffer. For most of its history, the NHLPA has had a singular focus: maximizing the earnings of its members. The problem is that virtually every other union has the same primary goal, but not at the expense of demanding the safest possible work environment for its constituents. The NHLPA's leaders always have claimed to only represent the players' wishes; even Paul Kelly, the most progressive NHLPA executive director, didn't choose to stress the visor issue. But with every passing year (and with each devastating injury), a neutral position becomes more difficult to justify.

San Jose Sharks defenseman Douglas Murray and Columbus Blue Jackets forward Ethan Moreau, both of whom dealt with significant eye injuries after not wearing a visor, made it clear there is no excuse for the continued reticence of players to protect themselves as best they can.

"Hockey players are idiots," Murray told reporters after the Malhotra injury (although he wasn't specifically referring to Malhotra). "You have to get hurt first so you know the value of it. That's what we do. I didn't put a visor on until I took a puck in the eye and scratched my cornea. You don't think you need stuff and then you add on as you hurt yourself. It's plain stupid."

Moreau, who suffered a serious eye injury when he played for Edmonton—and incredibly, chose not to wear a visor even after he was hurt—told *The Columbus Dispatch*: "There is no intelligent response as to why I don't wear [a visor] . . . There's really no argument against them. I've just played so long without one. I just like playing better without it. To say it affects the way you play isn't a great argument, either, because most of the best players in the world now wear visors."

Murray's reasoning does a good job of explaining why, even after the long list of players affected by eye injuries continues to grow, only 59 percent of NHLers were wearing a visor in the 2010–11 season. Granted, that number is a large improvement from the 15 percent of visor-wearers in the league in 1998–99. But the fact remains that four in 10 of the best hockey players on the planet are placing their sight and careers in the fickle hands of fate 82 nights a year.

That is entirely unacceptable.

And let's consider what these players are openly admitting here. Moreau said there is no valid excuse for not wearing a visor. However, these players don't think twice about removing the visor because nobody has confronted them with that truth and demanded that they wear one. If you give them the choice, some guys who are otherwise rational individuals will rationalize the choice to go without a visor. New York Islanders defenseman Bruno Gervais wore one from his childhood days through his junior hockey career through his NHL debut in 2005. However, in the 2010–11 campaign, he had his shield removed. Why?

"I just felt I could see a little better, and it's a mental thing, too," Gervais said. "I felt really comfortable without one. When I took it off, it felt nice. It didn't really work out like I wanted, though."

That's an understatement. On November 26, 2010, the newly visorless Gervais got himself into a fight with six-foot-four, 225-pound New Jersey Devils defenseman Colin White (who, ironically, had suffered a serious eye injury three years earlier). The six-foot, 188-pound Gervais was soundly thrashed as White fractured his cheekbone.

Despite that unfortunate series of events, Gervais continued to play without a visor when he returned to action a couple weeks later. But paradoxically, he acknowledges there is little logic in the action he's taken and wouldn't be upset to see the NHL grandfather in a mandatory visor rule.

"I don't think a grandfather rule would be a bad thing," he said. "The puck is shot a lot harder, and things move faster than ever before. And at the end of your career, you want to enjoy your time as much as possible. So I don't think wearing a visor is a bad thing at all."

As Murray said, NHLers are unaware of the true risks of eye injuries until they suffer one themselves. But the game no longer can afford to educate its players about eye protection via firsthand experience. For that matter, it never could afford it in the first place. As was demonstrated in the post-lockout obstruction crackdown, NHL players are able to adapt to what is asked of them. Continuing to find reasons not to ask them is another abdication of responsibility on the part of team owners, GMs, and members of the players' union.

● ● ●

You can't point to all the injuries listed in this chapter and say that all or even most of them would have been prevented if more stringent safety measures were in place. But expert doctors say that safety measures undoubtedly would have cut down on the overall number of injuries.

Whether that would've resulted in a longer NHL career for Pat LaFontaine, Paul Kariya, or Eric Lindros, or whether it would have spared the playing days of a simple member of the NHL working class such as Manny Malhotra or David Tanabe is immaterial. The fact that the game could have done so, could've lessened the burden on its most precious resources—its players—and instead shrugged its shoulders and yawned is the true outrage here.

So what is it that drives much of the acceptance of that philosophy? In short, it's a macho attitude that's rooted in male vanity. No player would ever admit to it, but the idea of playing without a shield or playing through all or any pain they encounter is all part of the romanticized psyche of the average NHLer. It's the same reason why bigger, bulkier helmet designs that may drastically increase the protection afforded to players' heads will always be silently sneered at by them. They prefer the sleeker, smaller look; Wayne Gretzky's famous helmet (made by Swedish manufacturer Jofa) was little more than a molded piece of plastic.

Because they haven't had it demanded of them, by their league and their union, players have been permitted to live in a bubble of their own making regarding their own value and safety—a bubble that allows them to imagine multiple concussions and their after-effects, or a life with just one good eye, could never happen to them. And every day that passes without a drastic change in that philosophy, every time the list of those lost to injury grows unnecessarily, represents another crushing blow to the bones of a sport that are already brittle enough.

FULL DISCLOSURE
MY OWN EXPERIENCE WITH HOCKEY VIOLENCE (OR WHY I HAVE MORE IN COMMON WITH TODD BERTUZZI AND MARTY MCSORLEY THAN YOU'D SUSPECT)

4

In the decade I've spent working at The Hockey News, *more than a few readers have gone out of their way to assign me a derogatory nickname or two. Those monikers are usually of the emasculating variety, and normally are accompanied by unsolicited advice directing me to lend my writing skills to what my detractors saw as more appropriate sports—croquet, badminton, men's doubles, freestyle nighttime snowboarding, that type of thing.*

I get that guff directed at me because I've never been shy to point out the wanton lunacy that occurs not only at the National Hockey League level, but all its North American feeder systems, right down to the amateur leagues where eight-year-olds have engaged in on-ice brawls, all in what passes as the pursuit of a victory.

Most of the criticism I deal with for holding that view is hilarious, not just for its predictability, but also for its simplicity. When people resort to personal attacks, it just confirms they can't argue the merits of their own philosophy. But that doesn't bother me at all. What truly upsets me is knowing that, each and every year, a steady stream of hockey players will be injured and the hockey establishment will find ways to excuse these injuries.

Year after year, I know I'll receive calls from TV and radio producers asking me to come on and comment about the latest act of inexplicable violence. Year after year, I know that players will suffer in the NHL and in rinks around the continent, thanks to a hockey culture that condones vigilantism and accepts catastrophic injury as an acceptable cost of doing business. Most times, the names of those involved and the body damage will vary, but the absence of reason and base-level sportsmanship—not to mention, the absence of appropriate punishment—almost inevitably remain the same.

Sometimes the weapon used is a stick, like it was when Marty McSorley belted Donald Brashear in his head and was disciplined with the longest suspension in NHL history (a suspension that essentially ended McSorley's career). Sometimes a skate becomes a makeshift revenge-delivery machine, such as when Chris Simon and Chris Pronger stomped down on their opponents in separate acts of temporary inanity. Sometimes, and especially in the fast-paced world of the NHL today, the body itself is the weapon; players hurtle themselves at opponents dozens of times each game. And sometimes it's simply a good old-fashioned assault à la fists that does something that, if done on the street or any other field of competition, would constitute sufficient physical harm to land the aggressor behind prison bars for more than a night or two.

No other sport exhibits such profound lack of respect for its participants the way North American hockey does. Other popular and physical professional leagues—in rugby, in football, heck, even in mixed martial arts—do not permit their athletes to collect and process evidence and dole out retribution as they see fit.

But North American hockey does.

• • •

Allowing players to self-police is shameful absentee ownership of a game masked in good ol' boy morality. It is okay when "We" do it, but never when "They" do it. For a sport that considers itself inherently Canadian, hockey has but trace amounts of the goodwill and common sense that drives its homeland in so many other venues. And it is, to the surprise of many who'll read this, something I experienced firsthand—not from the victim's side, but as the one doing the victimizing. Because, despite what low-wattage hockey traditionalists would love to believe, I wasn't the kid who had ice shards kicked in his face and his lunch money stolen by bullies. I was the bully doing the kicking and stealing.

That's right, all you knuckle-draggers, Don Cherry enthusiasts, and/or super-tough single-finger typists who are convinced I raised daisies on a hippie farm as a child: Adam Proteau used to be a hockey goon. I know—that's almost as shocking as any time Adam Proteau refers to himself in the third person. Adam Proteau typically finds that more than a bit egotistic.

Yet it's true. For much of my time on the ice, I was an aggressive, easy-to-antagonize, borderline predatory menace. In the particularly little pond in which my hockey community gathered, I was considered a good teammate, a hard worker, and someone the other team would have to answer to if liberties were taken with our more talented players. I'm sure my opponents saw it differently, but in my mind, I was the one who would avenge a teammate that had been wronged by a real bully.

For the longest time, I loved playing that role. But eventually, I was cast as a villain. And the way I left organized hockey—in the wake of an incident I'll elaborate on below—serves as the bedrock upon which I view the game today.

• • •

From the age of eight or so, I was the kid who was a-head-and-a-half taller than many of my teammates. In the Weston Minor Hockey League (a suburb of Toronto that's also been home to Paul Coffey, Mike Liut, and Craig Ramsay), I was an all-star.

Please don't take that to mean I was any good; judged against kids in my neighborhood, I knew how limited my skills actually were. But at the house league level, I was the kid traded from one really good team to one really cruddy team—and, insultingly enough, in return for a four-foot-eight kid who was the quintessential ankle-bender!—before the season even started, so as to even rosters out before games got lopsided and ugly.

What I lacked in skating fundamentals—and believe me, I lacked them fundamentally; my Scottish bowlegs could've served as bookends to a regulation-length sandwich board laid out horizontally—I compensated for with aggressive, highly physical play. It worked wonders for me, even as I began to realize I was a good-sized fish in a small pond.

And I didn't just love being one of the biggest kids on the team. I loved the game as much as anything else. My grandmother worked in the west-Toronto warehouse for hockey equipment maker CCM and would get me autographs from Leafs players like Laurie Boschman, John Anderson, and Rocky Saganiuk when they came by. I watched Howie Meeker and Gary Dornhoefer and Peter Puck on *Hockey Night in Canada*, and skated at the Easter Seals skate-a-thon at Maple Leaf Gardens, where I got to meet hockey legend Bobby Orr.

I went to Marlies games at the Gardens, watched my more talented friend Andrew Verner (who went on to a professional hockey career in Europe and was a draft pick of the Edmonton Oilers) at the AAA level. We also attended Leafs games when one of our fathers came through with tickets, and both of us traveled across the province to play in games whenever possible.

In my final year of organized hockey, I was named best defenseman for my age group in the Weston League. I was the master of the sliding, sweeping poke-check from behind (usually after my opponent blew past me) and I was decent enough at that modest level to be a solid selection for the local house league all-star team.

Because of my size and mean streak, I also was not to be messed with on the ice. And being that type of kid brought me face-to-face with the allure of sticking up for your teammates. Avenging wrongdoings done to your buddies was *mucho-macho* business; it carried with it an easily defined sense of purpose that was encouraged and reinforced by coaches and teammates, and combined with the far right overtones of the 1980s anyway (have you looked back upon a *Rambo* movie with any kind of perspective?), it was a highly sought-after skill.

More importantly, it was physically and emotionally exhilarating. It was a way to be fearless inside of a controlled environment. I was provider and protector on the ice—and it made me feel good about devoting so much time to the sport. That warm feeling of being a protector, of being there for your teammates in a primal, black-and-white way, is the same feeling NHL enforcers have at hockey's highest level.

"You know your teammates know what role you're playing and for sure it feels like you're helping the team when you're standing up for your teammates," said veteran NHL enforcer Georges Laraque. "If the other guys are out there taking advantage of you and you do something to let them know they can't keep doing that, of course your teammates are going to appreciate you doing that."

"Sure, it felt good to right a wrong," added former NHL tough guy Jim Thomson. "I never felt badly about going after someone I thought went after someone on my side."

• • •

Based primarily on my size and willingness to use it, I made it as high as single-A hockey, playing for Duffield of the North York Hockey League one season. There, I won an Esso "Medal of Achievement," albeit as the dreaded Most Improved Player, which showed you how awful a skater I was prior to even reaching that modest plateau.

So when I returned to Weston House League the following season for what turned out to be my final year, I was brasher and bolder than ever before. And although I didn't realize it at the time, I was a powder keg who would ignite and explode before the year was through.

The beginning of the detonation period took place one afternoon that season at my home arena—Weston Lions Arena, one of the best old-time rinks in Toronto, where many TV commercials and movies are shot for its retro feel—for a house league All-Star game.

At one point during the game, what started out as a minor scuffle on the ice quickly snowballed and turned into a full-on line brawl between the two teams. My "dance partner" when the music broke out was a kid much smaller than me. But he was armed with a tool of his own—his sneer of a smirk (or smirk of a sneer), which was maddening to a degree that made me shake him around the way NHL star Zdeno Chara once did former Leafs defenseman Bryan McCabe.

Because I had the size advantage on Mr. Sneer, I was quickly able to throw him down on the ice, flat on his back. But the fight was escalating—not only between me and my rival, but between everyone from both teams who wasn't on the resting side of the boards. And even some who were.

In a sideways, half-second glance, I saw our backup goalie dive—belly-flop-style, from his perch standing on the bench—onto a kid lying prone on the ice. It was hilarious and inspiring all at once.

I looked back down at the toad I'd throw around like a rag doll. He wasn't in any physical position to claim victory, as I was standing overtop of him, grabbing my stick off the ice from nearby. But I hadn't robbed him of any of his sneering veneer, either. Lying on his back looking up at me, he looked up and uttered two words that veterans of Legion establishments and long-haul transport will be very familiar with.

"Fuck you!" he said.

I don't know if it was the combination of his tone of voice and his smack-worthy face, but that sneer and that obscenity set off something in my mind that made me see red.

Like it was yesterday, I remember raising my stick up behind my head with both hands and bringing it down violently onto the kid's body. I think I got in three or four good whacks before the referee grabbed hold of me and pulled me away.

I was McSorley-on-Donald-Brashear 15 years before McSorley bashed Brashear in the head with his stick. I was Wayne-Maki-on-Ted-Green (another famous and ugly stick-swinging incident that took place in 1969) a decade-and-a-half after the former NHLer fractured the latter player's skull with his stick.

After the game, I found out my teammates on the bench were loving every second of my meltdown. But in the chaos on the ice, I could only hear one sound.

Boos. A lot of boos. In my home arena. Throaty, passionate, sustained boos, despite the fact there were only a handful of visitors occupying the stands. That felt odd to hear, especially in your home rink. Then I realized who was giving me the raspberry routine and that odd feeling turned into a sickly one. I was being booed by moms from my own team. (Not my own, thankfully; she was at home that day and my father was at the rink.)

I didn't think booing from moms on your own team was possible under any circumstances. I thought moms on your own team inherently understood that any serious action like the one I took was merited only because there was some underhanded chicanery going on.

So imagine how weird it was when I got into the dressing room and was greeted by my teammates. It was not dissimilar to any get-together wherein an oil baron enters a room full of politicians to play Money Santa, or when Oprah Winfrey leaves the house at any time. Giddy doesn't begin to adequately describe the prevailing sentiment among my fellow Weston all-star players. I was the conquering hero, Charles Bronson in a CCM helmet and Cooperalls (yes, I'm sorry to say) rolled into one. A teammate instantly nicknamed me "Hacksaw," after the famous pro wrestler who brought a two-by-four block of wood to the ring with him and swung it at opponents' heads.

I have no problem admitting I felt good on a base level in acting in defense of the team. My friends were making me re-enact the lumberjack job and we all laughed good laughs about it for the next few days.

But although I didn't know it, that was the beginning of the end of my days playing organized hockey.

After the game, I don't think my father knew how to react. He could see I was energized by the reception I got from my teammates, but he also was in the stands while parents around him booed me with all their lungs could give them. When we got home and my mom found out, she was more relieved I hadn't been hurt in the brawl than angered over anything I did in it.

Then came the suspension. I received an eight-game ban (in a combination of house-league and All-Star games) and I was sent an official warning on Metro Toronto Hockey League (MTHL) letterhead stating that any further egregious acts on my behalf would result in permanent banishment from the league.

Permanent. Banishment. The concept wobbled around inside my stomach, making me queasy, anxious, and embarrassed.

I was facing expulsion from my favorite game and estrangement from the friends I'd made. And for what? For something I was hailed as a hero for among the guys I played the game with. Those guys understood this slimy kid really must've done something to deserve what I gave him. They knew I wasn't being asked to play with my good side, but rather, for the good of my side. They felt like I was being made an example of, and I wasn't about to disagree.

But I bit my lip and served my time—while the legend of Hacksaw Proteau rapidly spread across my corner of Toronto—and when the suspension ended, I rejoined my All-Star teammates for a game at the old Lakeshore Lions Arena in West Toronto.

It didn't take the full 60 minutes of the game for me to be faced with the first test of my league-mandated, peace-loving mentality. I drilled an opponent into the boards with a check—one to which he quickly took exception. So the pushing started. And the f-bombs began dropping. And the gloves came off.

And that's when I remembered: *Permanent. Banishment.*

The words were as heavy as they were the first time I saw them on that MTHL letterhead. They jabbed into me like knives dipped in vinegar. In the blink of an eye, all I could imagine was sitting on the sidelines, fully healthy, but not being able to play. Not being *allowed* to play. I was stunned. So as my tormentor reared back in what seemed like slow motion and sent fist after fist into my swanky new clear iTech visor, I didn't punch back; I could see it coming, but I'd already taken the worst punch possible.

Wham! The guy drilled me square in the chops, squinting as he threw his weight behind the punch.

Wham! Wham! The next one sent my chin strap flying off to the side, and the one after that made it feel as if I was in a video boxing game.

Wham! Wham! Wham! I really began hoping one of the officials would arrive soon to intervene.

When one of them eventually pulled me out of the one-sided scrum, I heard different sounds coming from the stands. They were cheers—and from the same moms who booed me back during my Hacksaw Game—for showing restraint.

Yet when I got back to remove my equipment after the game, my teammates couldn't reconcile the new me with the Hacksaw they were just getting to adore and mythologize. They didn't turn their backs on me the way you'd see in some contrived Hollywood kids' movie. They understood why I didn't want to risk never playing again, but couldn't conceal a primal sense of dismay that one of the bigger bullies/policemen/revenge artists on the team had been effectively neutered.

To recap: when I was Hacksaw, I was deified by teammates—I honestly felt as if they wanted to carry me off the ice on their shoulders—and demonized by their parents. When I was a pacifist, the converse was true. They couldn't quite accept that the old me was now the new me who'd been made to stay behind a clearly defined behavioral line in the sand.

It never sat well with me. By the end of that season, I was conflicted and exhausted about how I'd come to feel toward the game. (I was also just heading into high school and soon would find myself pulled into other aspects of athletics, like swimming and, um, socializing.) I was still enjoying the camaraderie, but I couldn't shake the sense I'd lost the ability to know what was expected of me on the ice.

I distinctly remember putting my hockey bag away under the stairs for summer storage after that season and thinking, hell, I'll just take the next year of organized hockey off and maybe play for my high school team later on.

· · ·

Things didn't turn out that way. I never played organized hockey again after that (in part due to a wonky back) and found other ways to have fun. I never had the skill to be anything other than a hockey beer-leaguer beyond that time, but looking back, I can see how urgently I wanted out of that scene.

Of course, my love for the sport never completely went away. When I had the chance to write about it for what many still refer to as "The Bible of Hockey," *The Hockey News*, I rediscovered the weight and scope of its appeal. And suddenly, two guys fighting (especially two guys who, by and large, were only on the team to punch the other punchy guy) didn't do as much for me as it had a decade earlier when I was playing.

Rather, it was skill that drew me back into the game's clutches. It was players flying down the wing and lighting up a goalie on the short side, not some poor schmendrick losing his Chiclets and/or cracking the back of his bare head on the playing surface.

Now that I no longer was caught up in the culture, most hockey fights felt like distractions—or as I prefer to call them these days, "Dancing Bear Acts"—and I noticed that, strangely enough, you'd never see one-trick hockey fighters taking up valuable space on the ice at the most important times of the most important games.

Do you remember a fight defining the 1972 Summit Series? Did a scrap define the 1980 Miracle on Ice at the Lake Placid 1980 Olympic Winter Games, or Sidney Crosby's gold-medal winning marker at Vancouver 2010? Was the 1987 Canada Cup decided on the basis of a mutual pounding from Wayne Gretzky and Mario Lemieux?

Just to suggest anything of the sort proves the absurdity of the notion that a fight has any lasting value to a hockey game. All those famous events are crystallized in our minds because of displays of goal-scoring or goal-stopping talent, not the ability to crush an orbital bone or belt an opponent into semiconsciousness.

You rarely see goons play, let alone fight in the playoffs, because when the stakes are highest, coaches put on their most talented players, and those players are virtually never the ones who are the so-called "policemen" of the game.

The funny thing is, of all the NHLers I speak with, the enforcers are by far the best-humored and relate easiest to everyday fans. Their place in the game's pecking order keeps them humble, and though I don't think their roles have any place in hockey, I've heard too many stories from them and seen too many examples of the inherent stresses of their duties to not have a healthy respect for them as human beings.

• • •

Former longtime enforcer Georges Laraque understands the toll as well as anyone. He accepts all the physical anguish enforcers deal with as the cost of doing their business, but says the psychological effect of playing a hyper-aggressive role is a much tougher opponent.

"I'll tell anybody that the job I did is the toughest job in hockey—actually in all of sports," said Laraque, one of the most recognizable and good-natured enforcers in hockey history. "When guys agree to do this job, there are a million things going through their heads all the time. Who am I going to be fighting next? What's going to happen if I hurt a guy, or if he hurts me? What if I lose a few fights in a row—will I lose my job? That's what you're thinking about day and night, and some players have difficulty coping with it."

Laraque, who finished a 13-year NHL career with 1,126 penalty minutes in 695 regular season games, saw the May 2011 accidental death of 28-year-old former New York Rangers and Minnesota Wild enforcer tough guy Derek Boogaard (from a lethal cocktail of alcohol and the painkiller oxycodone) as an indication of the problems some players have with the job.

"Some guys have depended on alcohol to deal with it," he said. "Other guys may do other things. For me, if I hadn't put myself into doing community service work, I don't know what would have happened. But I had to do it—first, to show people that I wasn't a savage, and to show my personality. But there are guys who get so caught up in the world of hockey, they don't know how to take a step away from it."

"Listen, I'm not complaining about what I did," added former NHL enforcer Jim Thomson, who parlayed an ability to throw punches into playing alongside Wayne Gretzky with the Los Angeles Kings. "It was what I did and it got me into the greatest league in the world. But when I look back now, I would have loved to have been [former Kings teammate and elite goal-scorer] Tomas Sandstrom for a night. The pressure of going out and getting an assist or a goal—man, I would have taken that tenfold compared to the pressure of fighting."

By and large, enforcers like Laraque are not dumb men—at least, not to any greater degree than any other segment of society. Stu "The Grim Reaper" Grimson earned his law degree and did good work for the NHL Players' Association. Former Maple Leafs tough guy Tie Domi became a highly successful businessman off the ice. Brad May is an eloquent, business-minded guy who would've succeeded no matter what career he chose.

But they were given a chance to play hockey at the highest level possible, in return for what they believed at the time to be a fair price that would be taken on their body. In a column for Sportsnet.ca in 2009, Laraque explained how the worst part of the job happens between the ears and not at the end of somebody's fists.

"What might surprise some people is that the mental part of fighting can sometimes be tougher than the physical part," he wrote. "A lot of the time, fighting starts a couple days before the actual game. You look at the schedule and get really worked up because you have a game against a team that has a top tough guy and, mentally, that's tough.

"You think about the guy, you watch his fight on YouTube, you try to tell yourself it's going to be okay but it's not. No one can ever understand this pressure unless you're a fighter yourself . . . I used to not be able to sleep before games and I would sweat in the afternoon. It was not a good feeling. Sometimes I was even praying that the other guy—or even me—would be scratched so the fight wouldn't happen.

Boogaard, the former New York Rangers and Minnesota Wild enforcer, died from a toxic mixture of alcohol and oxycodone (a prescription drug he had abused in the months prior to his death). According to Laraque, the pressure to get himself back into the lineup after an injury was getting to Boogaard, who had just signed a lucrative, multimillion dollar contract with the organization in the summer of 2010. But for whatever reason—and the Rangers were aware Boogaard was seeking treatment for his oxycodone troubles—the team did not want him back in the dressing room so soon.

"He went to [the Rangers late in the season] and told them he was ready to come back," Laraque said of Boogaard, whom he had befriended and planned to train with in the summer of 2011. "They told him not to and to take the rest of the year off. Do you know what that does to a guy's mind? You sign him to a huge contract and less than a year later, he doesn't know what his future is gong to be with the team? That was a pretty brutal thing to do, in my opinion."

And that's another reason to challenge the role they play. As time goes by, and as we can see above, we learn more and more of the heavy toll fighting takes on enforcers both physically and psychologically.

• • •

If we really respect fighters and what they endure, we ought to be asking ourselves why we're okay dehumanizing them so that we can continue to see them place themselves in harm's way for our entertainment. While we're at it, we also ought to be asking why we lash out against extreme on-ice violence—and don't get me wrong, I think we should—then look the other way as other acts of aggression are perpetrated game in and game out.

Todd Bertuzzi, for example, was pilloried across North America for assaulting Steve Moore during an NHL game between the former's Vancouver Canucks and the latter's Colorado Avalanche back in March 2004. But—and in spite of the *sturm und drang* emotionality that painted him as the game's ultimate black hat—Bertuzzi also was victimized by the situation. Bertuzzi isn't even a goon in the traditional sense, as he's too skilled a player. He was reared in and rewarded by a hockey culture that encouraged guys to cross the line with regularity. A behemoth six-foot-three winger who could score, Bertuzzi played ornery and ugly when he first ran roughshod over the Ontario Hockey League in the early 1990s.

Bertuzzi was pushed and prodded and enabled by the hockey culture to bare his fangs, bark, and occasionally bite. In his first three seasons in the Ontario League junior system, he averaged 54 games played and 159 penalty minutes. He was accepted as someone who played "on the edge," which is hockey code for "this guy is allowed to go over the edge every so often." It took awhile, but his NHL career blossomed in Vancouver; in the 2002–03 campaign, he scored what will turn out to be a career-high 46 goals and 97 points. He was named to the league's First All-Star Team and played in two consecutive All-Star Games.

But then Bertuzzi finally snapped on the ice—coming up behind Moore and drilling him in the head, knocking Moore unconscious before he hit the ice, then piling his 230-pound body on top of Moore's—and the game ostracized him in an instant. He was the convenient, catch-all boogeyman, meant to distract from the core principles (or lack thereof) that made it possible for the tragedy to take place. And just like that, all the attributes that made Bertuzzi the apple of scouts' eyes as a young player were remade into a noose with his name on it.

When Bertuzzi made himself and the sport's culture vulnerable in the public spotlight through his actions with Moore, the hockey establishment pretended he was a savage and cast him out of its good books. The story behind the incident was that Moore, a workmanlike player who had to scratch and claw to make it to hockey's highest level, had leveled Canucks star (and Bertuzzi's close friend) Markus Naslund in the previous game, and that hockey's "code" dictated that someone on Vancouver had to make Moore pay with a physical beating.

In hockey's twisted sense of heroism, Bertuzzi was sticking up for a teammate. Undoubtedly, that's part of the reason why Wayne Gretzky picked Bertuzzi as a member of the Canadian Men's Olympic Team for the 2008 Salt Lake Games, but it didn't matter to an irate public: Gretzky was heavily criticized for including Bertuzzi, and the media and the public tore Bertuzzi's image to shreds.

After the one-season suspension he received—which many saw as a slap on the wrist, as the entire 2004–05 NHL season was canceled in a labor dispute—Bertuzzi was never the same player. Moore, who suffered a concussion and broken neck, was physically unable to continue his life as an NHLer. Bertuzzi was haunted by this fact, though he was able to do so from the comfort of an NHL career that continued. The incident was raised in virtually every story that has since been written on him, and he's never scored more than 18 goals in a single season since 2003–04.

His nightmare hasn't yet ended. Yes, he's back in the NHL and has played more than 300 games since he ended Moore's career—but the legal case against him has dragged on for years with no settlement, and with an expectation it will be heard before the British Columbia court system in late 2011 or early 2012. A sizable percentage of the millions Bertuzzi has made before and since has gone to the lawyers defending him, and he will wear the shame of his over-reaction long after he retires from the game.

To be sure, Moore suffered the most of anyone in GM Place that day in 2004. Bertuzzi, though, learned a painful lesson about fighting and the joy it eventually drains from those who excel at it. Even the ones who were good at what they did, like Laraque and Thomson, yearned to excel enough at the game in order to not have to fight.

"I could play the game," said Thomson, who also scored 23 goals and 51 points for the Toronto Marlies in his final year of junior hockey. "I could shoot the puck and score goals. But once you're slotted into a role, it's very tough getting out of the role. I'll give you an example: I was on a tear in the American League, player of the week, and I get called up to Washington. But there, I was a fourth-line fighter. And then I got traded to the Hartford Whalers and the fights went on and on."

"Would I have wanted more of an opportunity to help the team in other ways?" added Laraque. "Who wouldn't want that? But that was my job, and I accepted it as what I had to do to stay in the NHL."

● ● ●

In the more than 10 years I've reported on hockey, I've learned that the sport and cartoonish violence aren't inextricably attached, and that positive change to the game is not only possible, but absolutely necessary for its long-term survival. I've spoken to people from all corners of hockey—from those who've played it at its most elite level; to those who've coached and managed the best players on earth, not only for particular teams, but leagues as well; to those who cover the sport as members of the media; to those medical professionals who see the consequences of hockey's manifested manias.

And in talking to a growing number of them, I can see that, slowly, the truth is starting to sink in. More players are beginning to comprehend—through their own professional experiences, through the struggles of former teammates, or through the careers of their children—that there is such a thing as a price that's too much to pay. More coaches and managers are looking at the accumulating medical information on head trauma in the game and coming to terms with the need for change. They know that there are only a finite number of elite players who can be spread throughout hockey's current infrastructure, and that the continued cannibalization of talent winds up hurting the sport at all levels.

Most of us know hockey is a game that can't thrive without physical battles. The problem is, nobody has ever had the courage and resolve to demand that those physical battles be allowed to continue, while at the same time insisting on minimal levels of respect. The solution for the NHL is as simple as the one that was used in my case: the deterrent of severe punishment can and must force players to reconsider the essence of hockey and the ramifications irrational actions can bring.

If an NHLer knows he risks losing part of his career (and a sizable portion of his salary), you'd better believe he'll think twice about raising his elbow or fists, or serving as a human-projectile as he drills his opponent into the glass. He will demonstrate caution to a greater degree. How much greater really is up to the player himself, but a serious financial penalty will give him no option but to change. The answer also has to include drastically increased education of players as to their own health risks. It's a responsibility that should be shouldered by the NHL Players' Association as well as owners of pro teams and all international hockey bodies—and include independent doctors to prioritize players' well-being.

"There's a big education process that needs to happen," says former NHL defenseman and current NHL Players' Association executive Matthieu Schneider. "Doctors are still finding out new things and trying to find ways to treat head injuries. And the more players know, the more they're aware, and the better decisions they can make for themselves and for each other."

Those who say this can't be done are the same people who said the game didn't need fixing, that obstruction and the restriction of talent were what hockey was really all about. They see the game not as an organic, always-evolving entity, but as a ritual whose fundamentals are never to be deviated from. Of course, the quality of NHL hockey since Brendan Shanahan's suggested changes were implemented has improved, proving those people wrong. But the old-school element of the game remains, and is inescapably on a collision course with the forward-thinking policies of the rest of the world around us.

• • •

As a kid, I had to face that battle back at Lakeshore Lions Arena. I suppose I could've chosen to take my chances with the authorities and punch my adversary as hard as he was punching me. And I chose to keep playing, to tone down the aggression, to focus on other aspects of the game that rewarded skill. Similarly, hockey's gatekeepers have a crucial decision to make: implement real change in their own way, with people who understand the nuances of the sport; or sit back idly and vainly and proudly until a lawsuit and/or government legislation give them no choice but to do so. There's still time for those leaders to take advantage of their stature and power and exhibit a vision for the game that is inclusive, flexible, and compassionate toward players to a much greater degree than hockey has seen to this stage.

As the world saw during the obstruction crackdown that followed the 2004–05 lockout season, hockey is as organic as any garden, and can be shaped and landscaped like any green space. Thus far, though, hockey's garden has been allowed to grow wild and unsightly.

By weeding out these invasive strands of violence, by giving the game back to those who play it best, by setting out a distinct direction for the garden's care from this point forward, the game is guaranteed to be more presentable.

WHY HOCKEY HAS IT BACKWARD
(OR THE CODE, THE RULEBOOK RARELY USED, AND THE SUPPLEMENTARY DISCIPLINE PROGRAM THAT'S MORE MENTAL THAN SUPPLE)

5

NHL players will tell you that a great number of the on-ice philosophies governing fighting, eye injuries, concussions, and other safety concerns are not found in the league's official rulebook. Instead, those elements of the game (and others) fall under the jurisdiction of something known as "The Code." If you're unfamiliar with it, The Code is the umbrella term for an unwritten, supposedly sacred set of etiquette guidelines hockey players claim to adhere to on the ice. As you'll see in this chapter, very few of The Code's tenets are able to withstand any scrutiny. But, for decades, The Code has been fetishized and romanticized strongly, corporately, and consistently enough to have legions of supporters who swear by it today. The on-ice officials themselves could— and should—have more power to call the game by the league's written rules, but they have been systemically conditioned to give players far more leeway than athletes in other contact sports are permitted.

That doesn't mean The Code deserves to retain its status as a cornerstone of the game and its philosophy. To see why, let's examine some of The Code's more notable rules and demonstrate the inherent logical fallacies. In no particular order:

Rule No. 1: No Turtles Allowed

If you take aggressive actions and constantly crash into your opponents with reckless abandon, sooner or later you're going to be challenged to drop your gloves and exchange punches with somebody who thinks their honor needs defending. Sounds like a black-and-white solution—something akin to deciding disputes in the days of the Wild West, doesn't it?

Well, it isn't. The notion that you have to answer the challenge to fight if you play a physical style is one of the main rules of The Code. But as with virtually every rule in The Code, there's a class of player whose sole intent is to break it. In this case, the code-breaker is known as an agitator. His role is to taunt and prod a member of the opposing team—the more talented, the better—into taking a swing at him, but *without fighting back*, so the other team takes a penalty, giving the agitator's team the advantage in the form of a power play.

For example, Sean Avery—loathed in 29 NHL cities and one of the worst turtle-artists in recent memory—consistently enables his team to gain the upper hand, such that his New York Rangers team benefits from his play and endorses it every time Avery appears in a game wearing their jersey.

Now, if "old-school players" had their way and the NHL's instigator rule (preventing out-and-out line brawls and goonery) was repealed, players such as Avery would be forced to fight—or at least take a good, old-fashioned face-punching "like a man." But think of the optics of a game that openly embraced fighting to that degree. Even the very effective message-spinning tactics of Gary Bettman wouldn't be enough to prevent the NHL from being the laughing-stock of the professional sports league and near total-abandonment by the advertising and business community, to say nothing of the criticism the league would receive from fans and parents of children in hockey who emulated such behavior.

How do you discourage a player such as Avery from cheapening the game with his actions? The same way you discourage any other act: by levying sufficient fines and/or suspensions that hit the players where it hurts most—their wallets.

Rule No. 2: Whatever You Do, *Don't* Touch the Other Team's Captain

In short, any contact with the opposition's best and/or most valuable player is prohibited in the strictest sense. Markus Naslund was captaining the Vancouver Canucks in spring 2004 when Colorado Avalanche footsoldier Steve Moore knocked him unconscious with a borderline check. Canucks fans and players were incensed that anyone would have the temerity to lay a check on their leader.

For a sport that takes great pride in showcasing its tough players, hockey looks at its leaders differently. Almost always using the example of Edmonton's Wayne Gretzky being protected by world-class enforcers Dave Semenko and Marty McSorley, fight advocates argue the NHL's most skilled players are not to be subjected to any hit whatsoever, unless, like Avs legend, Hall of Fame center, and former Flyers captain Peter Forsberg, they played a physical game.

Naslund, an offensive dynamo from Sweden, was not that type of physical player. And so, a full 16 days after Moore's check, Vancouver winger (and Naslund's best friend on the team) Todd Bertuzzi—still seething from the hit on his friend and teammate—eventually sucker-punched Moore in the back of the head (another breach of The Code, by the way) in an attempt to make Moore accountable for violating The Code rule and checking the Canucks captain.

If not hitting a captain or very talented player was written into the official NHL rulebook, it would have given players like Forsberg—a tough-nosed player not above taking an after-the-whistle cross-check to the back of an opponent—the equivalent of diplomatic immunity on the ice. (Even then, Forsberg apparently always could get away with jamming the butt end of his stick into someone's ribs or slashing an ankle or two, but you could only hit Forsberg so hard before you had to answer to the goon who played on his team.)

While this rule of The Code is never going to be openly enforced for obvious reasons, it begs the question: why is it tolerated on an unspoken level? Sure, it's understandable that players don't want the other side taking liberties with one of their leaders, one of their meal tickets, or any teammate for that matter. But it's really up to the referees (and if necessary, the NHL's supplemental discipline department) to enforce fairness as best they can.

Of course, the NHL gives the players no confidence their grievances will ever be addressed, which is why players such as Bertuzzi take the law into their own hands.

Rule No. 3: No Checking from Behind

Take it to the bank—any time you see a player knocked head-first into the boards by an opponent, you will, within seconds, witness a multi-player melee. No one on either team will stop to ask questions; the play will occur, and then, like a lit match during a gas leak, there will be a terrible explosion of violence.

The most infamous example of a hit from behind came in late May 1996, when Detroit center Kris Draper was drilled into the boards from behind by Colorado Avalanche agitator Claude Lemieux during Game 6 of the Western Conference final. The hit, which took place at the end of the players' bench, sprung Draper's face straight into the top edge of the boards, breaking his cheekbone, jaw, and nose, and concussing him. *New York Times* writer Joe Lapointe said he "looked like the victim of a car accident. Two hours after the incident, blood still flowed from his mouth and nose. His cheeks were swollen."

Colorado went on to win Game 6, in the process eliminating the Red Wings from the playoffs. Draper required reconstructive facial surgery and had to have his jaw wired shut. Lemieux was suspended, but only for two games, and returned to action for Game 3 of the Stanley Cup final.

The following season, knowing how Wings fans and media were all but baying for Lemieux's head on a spike, the Avalanche failed to put him in the lineup the first three times the two teams played. But when Lemieux joined the lineup in the fourth game between the franchises (on March 26, 1997), Wings players were quick to show they had not forgotten—nor forgiven—his transgression. Within five minutes of the game's first puck-drop there was a fight. After 10 minutes, there were two fights. And then, at the 18:22 mark, all hell broke loose.

Red Wings enforcer Darren McCarty shook off a linesman's grasp and pummeled Lemieux mercilessly with his fists—as well as a knee to the head—as Lemieux lay on the ice protecting himself with his hands. As McCarty was hammering away on Lemieux, Avs goalie (and future Hall-of-Famer) Patrick Roy took off from his net and headed to break up the one-sided beating. Before he got there, Detroit forward Brendan Shanahan intercepted him in the middle of the ice with a body check, and Roy quickly thereafter got into a full-on fight with Detroit goalie Mike Vernon (see below for the Code rule that states goalies can only fight other goalies). Meanwhile, a wrestling match was taking place between Colorado's Peter Forsberg and the Wings' Igor Larionov.

An entire 15 seconds of play had resumed following that sequence of events before Avalanche right-winger Adam Deadmarsh and Detroit d-man Vladimir Konstantinov engaged in the final fight of the opening period. And when the second period began, it took all of four seconds before the Avs' Adam Foote and Shanahan squared off, followed by four more fights in that period. In total, there were nine fights in the game. The Red Wings beat the Avs where it actually counted, winning the game 6–5. Nobody learned anything, no behavior was corrected—Lemieux remained the same super-pest for his entire career—but The Code had been followed.

In many ways, the outrage over hits from behind is perfectly legitimate and understandable. More and more players are being seriously injured every year through such hits. As a result, more and more NHLers and fans want change. But that change must be delivered by the league and not by emotionally charged players involved in, or witness to, any melee.

When the NHL doesn't seriously reprimand players who cause injuries, either intentionally or otherwise, the injured and/or aggrieved feel there's no choice but to administer their own disciplinary action.

Rule No. 4: Goalies May Only Fight Other Goalies

As we saw in the Patrick Roy/Darren McCarty/Brendan Shanahan/Mike Vernon case above, there's a reason why goaltenders very rarely fight a player other than a fellow goaltender. The Code says it's not allowed. Of course, there are exceptions to the rule. More recently, former Ottawa Senators goalie Ray Emery (a boxing aficionado) happily engaged in a fight with former Buffalo Sabres enforcer Andrew Peters. But 99 times out of 100, a netminder will go after his fellow goaltender.

Why? Well, because goalies fighting in the first place is a distinct rarity in pro hockey. They aren't all built like brick wall enforcers, so they're not physically capable of holding their own against anyone other than a fellow netminder. And they're so important to the team's chance of winning that coaches, GMs, and owners would quickly rid themselves of any goalie who showed a propensity for charging out of his crease and risking injury. Moreover, think about what fighting proponents tell you: "It's a spur-of-the-moment thing!" they say. "Pure emotion, from guys bumping into each other at high speeds all the time!"

If that is true, how could two goalies—each at opposite ends of the arena all night, each with masks that hide virtually all their emotions—possibly work up sufficient animus to charge the length of the rink and begin swinging at each other? Is there a more phony, soulless exercise in the sport today? Not in my opinion. And given how valuable most teams consider their goalie to be, why on earth would any franchise put their well-being at risk just for the sake of a fight?

Before you throw out the "nobody gets hurt in a fight" argument, consider the fight that occurred between New York Islanders netminder Rick DiPietro and Pittsburgh Penguins counterpart Brent Johnson on February 2, 2011. DiPietro first went after Matt Cooke (surprised to see Cooke's name in there, aren't you?), then left the ensuing scrum and faced off with Johnson, who had moved down to the Isles' blue line to challenge him. The two goalies had barely removed their equipment when Johnson threw the first punch—an over-hand left that caught DiPietro square on his right cheekbone. DiPietro, an often-injured player (who was supposed to back-stop the franchise for a decade or more when the Isles signed him to a 15-year, $67.5 million contract in 2006), dropped instantly to the ice. He was conscious, but clearly beaten. And after he got back to the dressing room, the doctors told him he had several broken bones in his face and would be sidelined for four to six weeks.

By The Code's standards, DiPietro did what he was supposed to do. Someone challenged him to a fight, and he accepted. However, as a direct result of that act, the Islanders lost his services for an extended period of time. So who benefits here? Certainly not the Islanders. And certainly not DiPietro. The Code doesn't pay DiPietro's salary, nor does it have a jersey that fans put their money behind and pour their emotion into. The Code didn't draft or develop DiPietro. But somehow, The Code takes precedence over everything else. Prepare for furrowed brows and expressions of bafflement if you try explaining this to any athlete or fan of other sports.

Rule No. 5: Demonstrate Proper Form

This concept manifests itself in many ways. For some players, it means waiting until a player has removed his helmet before the fight begins; for others, it means fighting someone either your own height and/or weight, or with a similar skill set. (For example, third-and-fourth-line players do not fight first-or-second-line stars.) Therein lies the biggest problem with the rule: it is as nebulous as they come.

Consider Montreal Canadiens rookie P.K. Subban, who was criticized by Toronto Maple Leafs winger Joffrey Lupul in February 2011 for not waiting until Lupul removed his helmet and visor before throwing punches.

"It's a pretty standard move when you both have visors on to take them off and [fight]," Lupul told reporters after the game. "He's a good, young player but his name keeps coming up over and over again [around the league]. I'm telling you, eventually guys are going to stop giving him the benefit of the doubt."

In Subban's defense, what was he supposed to do? Willingly absorb one or two punches to the face simply to ensure Lupul was completely prepared for the scrap? Using that logic, maybe the referees should check both players for foreign objects like brass knuckles before the fight—like they do in another utterly contrived act known as pro wrestling.

As for the idea that you need to be an almost perfect physical match for an opponent before taking him on—doesn't that also sound like the system used by boxing? If fighting is about split-second spontaneity as many claim, how could any NHLer—in the thick of the on-ice action—decide who does and doesn't fit the appropriate profile?

Rule No. 6: When You Score, Do Not Exhibit an Ounce of Joy

In the NFL, a touchdown is usually followed by an end-zone celebration that often includes a player jumping into the stands to celebrate with fans, or a rehearsed and short dance pantomime sequence or two. For obvious reasons, those things aren't possible in a sport whose players have steel blades attached to their feet. But the NHL is about as far as can be from the NFL when it comes to athlete celebrations on the field of play.

The Code for celebrations can be encapsulated in three short steps: (1) Score goal; (2) Turn around, skate to bench, and politely tap gloves with teammates; (3) Complete steps 1 and 2 while remaining as outwardly joyless as possible.

Now, imagine what a six-or-seven-year-old kid thinks when, after a goal, he sees his favorite NHLer move as a government bureaucrat does in filing a citizen complaint. The message that kid sees is "just another day on the job." When compared to other modern sports such as snowboarding and extreme games, where athletes smile and high-five all day long, the NHL comes off as a staid, happiness-free game in the mind of that child who's watching. Alas, when it comes time to divvying up his disposable income, not to mention his time and emotion, which sport do you imagine that kid will choose to buy into?

Hard-core hockey traditionalists will tell you that scoring celebrations humiliate opponents, and those opponents will use anything—a smile, a wink—as a motivator toward improving their play and having a better chance of beating the team that did the scoring in the first place. Better, say those traditionalists, to look nearly glum after a goal and let the opposition stay calm. This philosophy never seems like the bravest thing for an athlete or coach to admit to. In effect, they're saying they fear the possibilities of a more motivated opposition. But shouldn't a team be able to deal with any extra motivation from the other side and win anyway?

Rule No. 7: Visors Are for Little Girls and Eunuchs

This one's pretty self-explanatory. And, as we've covered in Chapter 3, this rule has been the cause of dozens of needlessly incurred, often career-ending injuries. And why? In part because of some small perceived advantage in vision, but mainly because of the inconvenience of in-game visor maintenance and NHLers wishing to avoid the feminized stereotype of a gutless player waving his stick around because he's more protected than his visorless (and apparently more respectful) opponent. But as noted throughout this book, if the problem with visors is that they make players more reckless, the way you address that is to increase the penalties, fines, and suspensions levied on those players—not to move in the other direction and refuse to mandate eye protection for every player on the ice.

In short, the idea a player is better and/or more responsible without a visor has never been proven. But those athletes who lose an eye, or have their careers hindered because of a serious or debilitating injury, could easily be painted as irresponsible.

Rule No. 8: Above All Else, "Respect" and "Honor" Your Opponents

Another amorphous blob of a concept, the notion that players somehow respect each other less today than they did before is complete nonsense. Apparently, we're supposed to believe players from the 1940s and 1950s politely tipped their fedoras at one another before a game and after every period, and never seriously jeopardized the well-being of the opposing team's players. As we covered previously, that is not the truth of the matter. In fact, one famously tough current player feels a little more strongly:

"That's bullshit," said Ian Laperriere, longtime NHLer and the recipient of *The Hockey News'* award for toughest player in the league in 2009–10. "Hearing that is one thing I'm tired of. When I started out playing, players were very rough on each other. If you compare that to today, there's no way at all you can say players care less now than they did in the past."

Indeed, you can make a good argument that players are *more* respectful today than ever before. In the so-called "good old days," NHLers didn't have the NHLPA and changed teams far less frequently (and thus never bonded with anyone outside of their own organization). It wasn't at all difficult, then, to incite hatred for a team or a specific individual.

• • •

So that's The Code. By contrast, the actual NHL rulebook is a public, fully acknowledged collection of league notions, some of which might as well be buried in dust for the amount of times the rules are actually called by the officials.

To wit: the reality is that charging—a penalty called regularly in the 1970s and 1980s when a player skated directly into an opponent at top speed without regard for the puck—has become acceptable behavior in today's NHL. Referees will not call the penalty because the directive to do so from head of officiating Terry Gregson (who takes his marching orders from commissioner Gary Bettman, who takes his direction from team owners) has never been made explicit to them.

The same was once true of hooking and holding penalties in what was known as the "clutch-and-grab" era. Referees saw all of it, but followed the league's orders and kept their whistles tucked away. The game suffered and the players suffered, but nothing was done to fix the problem until after the 2004–05 lockout season. Once officials were given the green light to crack down on obstruction, they followed through—consistently enforcing the rule and improving the product exponentially.

If you remember what the NHL did when Sean Avery ran afoul of the league in a playoff game in 2008 (waving his stick directly in the face of Devils goalie Martin Brodeur), you'll know the league can change a rule any time. In that case, the rule was unsportsmanlike conduct. And the turnaround time it took to change that rule was less than one day. And just like that, without any test marketing in the American League, without any extended debate from the NHL Board of Governors or the NHL Players' Association.

Such is the power that is held by the league and the league alone. But that power has never been used—purposefully—because the league sees injuries and chaos as inseparable from its overall product.

"One of the things that's important is that we want to keep the fundamental aspects of our physical game but at the same time protect the players," NHL commissioner Gary Bettman said at the 2011 All-Star Game, not realizing the contradictions inherent in that statement. "I don't like the fact that any players don't play or miss games because of concussions. But keep in mind our teams have, collectively, about 800 players. There's 1,230 regular-season games. We have over 50,000 hits and about 75,000 minutes of playing time. Of course, the ideal number of concussions would be zero. And our objective is to come as close as possible to getting that result *without changing the fundamental nature of our game* [emphasis added]."

See what he does there? The words "fundamental aspects/nature" and "physical game" are used as a protective umbrella against the outrage that rains down on the league from fans and media sick and tired of watching players lost at a sickening rate.

• • •

The other element at play in deciding player behavior is the supplemental discipline program headed by NHL vice-president of hockey operations Colin Campbell until June 2011, when he stepped down as chief disciplinarian and handed the duties over to former NHL star Brendan Shanahan. One of the main problems with the NHL's unpredictable suspension process is the priority the league puts on whittling down suspensions. In essence, the NHL finds any excuse it can to take a potentially lengthy suspension and excuse it down to a mere one-or-two-game ban.

By contrast, other professional sports leagues look at a player's misdeeds as reason to ratchet up the supplemental discipline.

In the NBA, Ron Artest got an 86-game suspension for a 2004 fight that spilled into the stands in Detroit and included fans. His teammate Stephen Jackson got 30 games in the same brawl. Kermit Washington was suspended 60 days (26 games) for a sucker-punch that nearly killed Rudy Tomjanovich and ultimately ended his playing career. In 2006, Denver superstar Carmelo Anthony got a 15-game ban for a single punch.

In the NFL, players are ejected immediately from any game in which they fight. They're also subject to fines like the $25,000 fines given to two players during the 2010 season (no NHLer has ever been fined for a straight-ahead fight). And in egregious cases, they could be subject to suspensions or even permanent expulsion from the league.

Excuses and character witnesses make no difference to those organizations; the act is what's being punished, and if there is enough malice (accidental or intentional), the punishment is heavy.

Not so with the NHL.

Another instance of that institutionalized ambivalence toward unruly behavior was found in the 2011 post-season, when Canucks agitator Raffi Torres (a player suspended for the final two games of the 2010–11 regular season and the first two games of the playoffs for a head hit to an opponent) slammed in to Blackhawks defenseman Brent Seabrook during the opening round playoff series between Vancouver and Chicago.

It seemed as if it was going to be an easy call to suspend Torres for longer than the four games he'd received only weeks earlier, especially as: (1) he had hurtled his body at Seabrook with no attempt to take control of the puck; (2) contact with Seabrook's head was undeniable; and (3) Torres was a repeat offender along the lines of Matt Cooke and Trevor Gillies.

As longtime observers have come to expect, Torres received no supplementary discipline whatsoever for the Seabrook hit. Campbell attempted to justify the decision by stating, "This hit meets none of the criteria that would subject Torres to supplemental discipline, including an application of Rule 48: he did not charge his opponent or leave his feet to deliver this check. He did not deliver an elbow or extended forearm and this hit was not 'late.'"

Similarly, Philadelphia Flyers captain Mike Richards twice escaped any kind of supplemental punishment for his actions in the first round of the 2011 playoffs. Playing against Buffalo in Game 4, Richards elbowed Sabres antagonist Patrick Kaleta in the head. The act landed Richards a five-minute major penalty during the game, but once again—and in spite of the play happening when (a) Richards already was infamous for his 2009 blindside hit on Florida's David Booth; and (b) the NHL publicly said it would toughen its approach to headshots—the league failed to suspend or even fine him. Then, in Game 6 of the Sabres/Flyers series, Richards drove the head of Buffalo center Tim Connolly into the boards. This time, Richards only received a two-minute penalty for boarding. The 29-year-old Connolly, who has struggled to cope with numerous head injuries during his NHL career, was knocked out of the game by Richards and wasn't able to play in Game 7 of the series.

Now, I'm not here to tell you Richards is a dirty player. In my dealings with him, I've found him to be an honorable guy and someone you'd want as your teammate. But he has been conditioned by the predominant hockey culture to push the boundaries and hit to hurt on the ice. If the league were truly serious about changing the predatory culture that robs it of so much talent, it is simply unacceptable that Richards should've come out of those two incidents (three, if you include the Booth hit) scot-free.

Yet, that is standard operating procedure at NHL head-quarters. Nobody seems to mind that, with every missed opportunity to set a standard for player behavior, the league sows the· seeds of conspiracy theories in the minds of fans who see their own player waylaid and the victimizer skate away without repercussion. And nobody at the NHL seems to care that the league's constant rationalizations of its lapses in judgment only embolden NHLers to carry out revenge on each other—and in the process, continue the cycle of revenge.

• • •

For nearly 30 years, Kerry Fraser was one of the most promi-nent, recognizable referees employed by the NHL. He knows all about The Code, and says most of it is hogwash. In particu-lar, he finds it laughable that people to this day are still trying to have the instigator rule repealed and, in effect, arguing the NHL's so-called "policemen" could do a better job of keeping players in line than officials or the rulebook.

"It's absurd, and that premise just boggles my mind," Fraser says. "Imagine if people said you could make driving a car safer by making everyone remove their seatbelts. You'd be laughed at. Maybe we should have the players take off their helmets and equipment while they're at it. The line of think-ing just doesn't make any sense whatsoever with me."

Fraser, who retired at the end of the 2009–10 NHL season and now serves as a TV analyst for TSN, doesn't believe the answer to the NHL's violence issue is putting more policing power in the hands of the players. He too thinks the best deterrent is a sharp increase in the dollar amount of fines and the length of suspensions. And, he thinks the league must take a big step back and do a better job of delineating what qualifies as illegal play.

"The officials are so confused, they don't know what is or isn't a penalty," says Fraser, 58, who officiated more than 1,900 regular-season games and 260 playoff games. "That's just the reality of it. And that confusion stems from public statements Colie [Colin Campbell] has made as to what is and isn't acceptable. Go back to [the 2009–10] season—[Capitals star] Alex Ovechkin gets suspended two games for cranking [Hawks defenseman] Brian Campbell into the boards from behind and breaking his shoulder. But then you go to [Hawks star forward] Marian Hossa in Game 5 of the 2010 playoffs. He gets a five-minute penalty against the Nashville Predators for boarding [Preds defenseman Dan] Hamhuis from behind, an act that was worse than what Ovechkin did. And then Hossa ends up stepping out of the penalty box and scoring the game-winning goal in the same game. How do you say that hit wasn't worth as much?"

During his officiating days, Fraser had a very simple, if subjective (as all officiating calls are, ultimately), manner to discern a match penalty that resulted in the immediate ejection from the game of the offending player. That standard, he said, is broken regularly.

"From my history," Fraser says, "if anything happened on the ice, no matter where it was, my litmus test was two words. If I saw a play and I went, 'holy f%#&!' that was a match penalty. That was bad. When Tiger Williams charged at Randy Holt in Washington in 1982 and snapped his stick on the back of Randy's helmetless head, that's a 'holy f%#&!' play. This year, you see the Raffi Torres–Brent Seabrook hit, and when you see Torres jump at Seabrook—who's not looking, not aware, he's looking for the puck—that's the type of play I'm talking about. But Torres goes unpunished. It's not justifiable, in my opinion."

Ultimately, Fraser feels as many progressive hockey minds do—namely, that the NHL needs to severely ramp up its supplemental discipline process and leave players, coaches, GMs, and on-ice officials with no illusions regarding the direction in which the sport has to go.

"With Colin Campbell, it [was] more about trying to find reasons not to call something or not to suspend people, and not holding them accountable for their actions," Fraser says. "That's where it's all falling apart. The deterrent isn't there. It's not about the players self-policing. You have to make it clear to players there's a serious price for the reckless actions we're seeing these days."

• • •

By looking at The Code, the actual NHL rulebook, and the intellectually backwards leaps the NHL must continually make to reconcile the two, it is easy to see how far hockey still has to go, simply to be on equal footing with the other professional sports leagues when it comes to the logical application of athlete behavior standards.

However, to start that process, the NHL has to admit what is plain as day. It must acknowledge that although nearly each and every one of the principles of The Code stem from admirable hockey values of courage and fairness, the problem at the core of each rule is that the players are the ones who are cast as plaintiffs, defendants, judges/juries, and executioners.

The NHL's administrators, who should be the ones playing the last two roles in the above scenario, are happy to sit on the sidelines and count the league's profits, only intervening in the most innocuous ways when the pesky media or fans voice their disgust over an incident. That has to change—and can, if fans make their voices heard, either by bombarding NHL head-quarters with their disgust over the problems, or by speaking with their wallets and refusing to attend games or buy league merchandise.

As well, Gary Bettman and the owners who give him his corporate marching orders have to insist on tougher punish-ments for repeat offenders and not pull back and whittle down those punishments when self-interested owners or GMs trot out tired old clichés meant to absolve players of their personal responsibilities on the ice. Until now, owners have been con-tent to count their hockey-related profits and view fighting as a necessary evil in selling the game. But as we see during playoffs and seminal hockey moments like the Olympics or World Championship tournaments, the game doesn't need that nutritionless filler.

The Code isn't doing anyone in hockey any favors. Well, that's not true—it does favors for those over-aggressive players who use it as a shield against logic, fairness, and sportsman-ship. But the price players pay to give those excitable, often less-talented players that excuse is far too high to let The Code continue.

Bettman once prefaced a Sean Avery suspension (that he got for merely saying the words "sloppy seconds") by invoking the league's responsibilities to parents who would have to explain the tasteless term to their children. To be sure, that is an admirable line of thought. But then try and explain to kids the essence of The Code. Try rationalizing a belief system that says it is not OK for a hockey player to smile after his team scores a goal, but it is more than OK—it is *demanded*—that hockey players always avenge anything they perceive to be a slight by hitting an opponent as hard as they can with a bare fist.

It simply can't be done. In sum, The Code is a relic that needs to be buried as soon and as deeply as possible.

HOCKEY ON THE BRAIN

HEALTH EXPERTS ON THE REPERCUSSIONS OF ON-ICE HEAD INJURIES AND VIOLENCE

You hear a number of common phrases used in hockey/NHL circles, and lately, you tend to hear a couple in particular mentioned again and again. One of them is, "This is a dangerous sport"; the other is, "Players understand what they're getting into when they choose to play this game at the professional level."

Nobody can question that hockey is a dangerous sport. Even with the harshest supplementary discipline punishments and state-of-the-art protective equipment, we're talking about a sport that uses steel blades to turn mere men into Mack Trucks, a sport whose players carry large sticks and long memories, a sport that has no out-of-bounds on its playing surface.

But in our modern world, where advertising campaigns for soft drink and potato chip products have diminished the impact of words like "dangerous" and "extreme," the tendency among hockey players is to shrug their shoulders and not give any serious consideration to the true dangers that exist for them in their line of work.

They are decent young guys who see themselves as being paid very handsomely because they've learned to minimize and look beyond the negative obstacles placed before them on their road to the NHL, and instead find the positive in any situation to help them continue their battle and push themselves to better days and paydays. Unfortunately, there are no positives or better days when it comes to serious brain injuries. (In fact, if you think you can argue there are benefits to head injuries, you may be suffering from one yourself.) So when people argue that pro players truly understand all that's at stake for them every time they step on the ice, I have to disagree—and disagree vehemently. In terms of their own health and well-being, in terms of their ability to avoid a substandard quality of life following their hockey career, NHL players haven't the faintest notion of what they're getting into.

In fact, for the most part they're often as in the dark as are those who suffer concussions.

"Players know what they're getting into with headshots? Come on," says former NHLer Keith Primeau. "I'd have to say that's a pretty ignorant statement. Players love the game and they're good at the game. And besides, the doctors are still trying to get a handle on head issues and concussions. They're researching and learning new things all the time, so to say players have a good idea of what's at risk—that's just not true whatsoever. That's ridiculous."

Since he retired, in part due to head injuries, and began working to promote awareness of the issue, Primeau has learned the smartest among us are only now beginning to scratch the surface of what is known about concussions and the human body in general. But the medical advances that have been made pertaining to the knowledge of hockey injuries always seem to make doctors more alarmed for the well-being of players.

In particular, clinical studies are shedding a brighter light on the delicate nature of the human brain—and the more that's discovered regarding concussions, the more concern grows in the medical community for the well-being of hockey players.

In many ways, the message from doctors is similar to that from those who observe the history of hockey in general: although the NHL and the professional side of the sport have made significant strides from where they once were, the league and the North American hockey industry still have much progress to make if they truly wish to be proactive and progressive in reducing the number of injured athletes.

"We've made progress, definitely, in terms of the sport and also in terms of the medical profession," says Dr. Michael Cusimano, a leading Canadian neurosurgeon and brain trauma professor and researcher at the University of Toronto. "When I first began talking about the headshots issue around 10 years ago, my own colleagues were ostracizing me. And now I think most of my colleagues are on the same team. I think the public has moved forward quite a bit as well. But I think there's still a ways we have to go."

In a 2011 study on the effect of body checking on youth playing hockey, Cusimano and his team of researchers found that, over the course of 10 years, more than half of the 8,552 reported hockey injuries (4,460, or 52.2 percent) were suffered due to body checking. He has long recommended a full-on ban of intentional body contact in youth hockey—advice Hockey Canada finally picked up on when, in May 2011, they announced all house league and house-league all-star players in Canada would no longer be subjected to body checking. (So called "rep-level" youth players—the kids who eventually have a shot at the NHL—still play a game with body checking in it.)

But there has to be improved protection for players at every level of the sport—protection for the kids who excel at the game and become fortunate enough to play it for a living, as well as for the young teenagers who aspire to play in the best leagues around.

Evidence of the need to protect professionals could be found in another recent medical study, this one from April 2011, that used actual NHL data to report on the causes and effects of head injuries suffered by players. From 1997–2004, the study found that 559 concussions were reported by NHL doctors—an average of 80 per season. In a league that has a handful less than 800 players, having more than a full 10 percent of players potentially suffering an injury has to send off warning bells—at least, under a responsible administration. And a full 20 percent of those 559 players reported they dealt with amnesia in the aftermath of the initial injury.

In addition, the study recorded that all but 30 of those cases resulted in players losing playing time due to concussions, including 31 percent of players who were sidelined for more than 10 days of competition. The study also found that players who suffered a second or third concussion had their subsequent recovery time increase 2.25 times on average with each additional hit to the head. In other words, one in 10 NHLers had to deal with a head injury every season, and that high percentage increased the likelihood a player would suffer more than one concussion and be sidelined for a significant period of time.

Contrast that to the NFL, where a 2000 study surveyed 1,090 former NFL players and found (a) more than 60 percent suffered at least one concussion in their careers, and (b) 26 percent had three or more. Seven years later, a study conducted by the University of North Carolina's Center for the Study of

Retired Athletes found that of 595 retired NFL players who had three or more concussions, 20.2 percent said they had been found to have depression. That number was three times the rate of players who have not sustained concussions.

So you can see that the problem of head injuries isn't the NHL's alone. But the NFL has moved rapidly to address some of the plays that lead to concussions. And one of those choices—especially the decision to ban helmet-to-helmet hits and hits on defenseless players and levy fines up to $75,000 for repeat offenders like Pittsburgh Steeler James Harrison—have led to some people questioning whether the NFL was too heavy-handed in attempting to enforce its rules.

NFL executive vice-president Ray Anderson, however, spoke about the issue like a true leader should.

"If there's one key message, it's that we will not relent in protecting player safety," Anderson said in 2010. "We've got a responsibility toward health and safety that just doesn't impact the NFL game. It impacts the college game, the high school game and the youth game. We are the platform. We are the role model for being aggressive about safety standards.

"We are at that point where we have got to [act] with all of the appropriate attention on concussions and head hits that are negatively impacting not just professionals but college players and youth-level players in all sports. Times have changed. If we have to face the backlash from those who will say we are making the game too soft, then so be it."

As for the NHL's insistence that a suspension can be calculated based on the offending player's intent? Anderson doesn't buy that, either.

"When something happens, everybody says they didn't mean to do it," Anderson said. "But if someone runs a stop sign and collides with another car, their intent might not be to cause any damage. But they are still accountable."

Meanwhile, in the NHL, players were being mowed down regularly and careers were being shortened on a predictable basis with no impetus on the league's part to address some of the key concerns But remember, the NHL is about "tradition" and is a "man's game" and values its brand of "physicality" more than anything else. As such, the league never moves quickly enough to wrestle down a growing menace. And thus, a steady stream of guys fell by the wayside each year, until Sidney Crosby's career was jeopardized and the hockey world was forced to focus on what doctors like Cusimano are now calling an epidemic.

"At rink side—by which I mean in the hockey community at large—there's still a lack of clear understanding as to what the real issue is," says Cusimano, who consults on several concussion-focused projects. "This is a cultural issue we're dealing with, and it takes a long time to truly change a culture. It's rare you get rapid-change kind of events in hockey. But something like the injury to Sidney Crosby can be a tipping point for awareness and action. Hopefully this wakes more people up to the problem that exists."

Working out of St. Michael's Hospital in Toronto, Cusimano sees patients who are far from the NHL limelight—kids playing for fun or in above-average (but not elite) amateur leagues, suffering brutal head injuries that can ruin their quality of life forever. Because of concussions, some of those kids can't take university tests or classes because they can't be in a room with fluorescent lighting for long periods, if at all. Some can't work because of constant migraines or lapses in focus. For their simple love of the game, they've been burdened with troubling medical issues that have no cure. Those are the kids Cusimano keeps in mind when advocating for immediate change to hockey's approach to headshots.

"I don't want to minimize the NHLers who've suffered head injuries, but the problem is this huge sea of youth who are suffering these effects and who'll never have stories written about their plight," Cusimano says. "The real problem is the kids who emulate NHLers. Kids look up to the big leagues to define what's right to do. They're influenced by the NHL to a large extent. But nobody cares about a 17-year-old who never will be in the NHL, yet has the rest of his life changed. They can ruin their ability to go to university and earn a proper living. Why are we doing this to these poor kids?"

Cusimano believes that part of the problem with the North American game's culture is the indoctrination Canadian kids, parents, and coaches receive at the hands of former NHL coach and popular CBC broadcaster Don Cherry every Saturday night during his first-intermission show on *Hockey Night in Canada*.

"This particular type of hockey culture does get promoted by certain forces in our society," Cusimano says. "The idea players are taught, that one is more of a man for playing through pain, is all-pervasive and is promoted by people like Don Cherry. When Don Cherry says something on *Hockey Night in Canada*, one million people hear it; of those one million, 300,000 are kids and the others have a link to the game in some manner. So immediately, someone like Cherry has a huge impact."

Like many physicians who study head injuries in hockey, Cusimano speaks like a man utterly baffled by the muted response to the crisis. He cannot fathom that custodians of the sport are not doing their utmost to cut down on concussions, regardless of the relatively trivial effect doing so would have on the game.

"There's no one who wins when a player induces an injury on a fellow player," Cusimano says. "Did the fellow who hit Crosby, did that help his team win or get him a big contract? No. He didn't really benefit at all. Ultimately, the whole game will lose from things like this. What is happening already is that players are leaving the sport, and the game is losing kids when they're 12, 13, 14 years old—right at the time they need to be physically active. But can you blame parents for pulling their kids out of the sport? Why on earth would anyone want their child to have a brain injury?"

Cusimano counts himself a fan of hockey, but recognizes that appreciating the game doesn't mean accepting the NHL's version of it.

"In the long run, hockey authorities allowing this type of behavior does nothing to benefit the sport," he says. "It's this contorted definition of what success is in hockey. Isn't success defined as the participants having fun? Isn't it about kids learning team play? About developing long-term friendship? About physical fitness? Aren't all those things why we want kids playing the sport? To me, those are the wins—not the score at the end of the game. Not leaving your opponent in a terrible condition."

• • •

One of Cusimano's colleagues and associates, Toronto-area neurosurgeon Dr. Neilank Jha, also cares deeply about the health of young hockey players and young athletes in general. He is arguing a different angle of the issue—namely, the need for a combined, nationwide effort to educate all Canadians on the growing menace that concussions represent.

"If you look at the NHL and what's happened with Sidney Crosby, it's not good for the league, the Pittsburgh Penguins, the player, anybody," says Jha. "What I'm advocating is that, while it's great for organizations like the NHL and people to govern themselves, it's unreasonable to expect them to be able to appropriately govern themselves if they don't have the awareness and knowledge available to them. It's not only the players who aren't aware—it's medical professionals like myself. There's a lot of instances in which I speak to people who've gone to family doctors regarding head injuries, and the doctor has been reluctant to send the patient back to playing the game, even when the injured person has gone through the correct steps to get back into the game. So the appropriate messages aren't getting out there to everyone, the way we need them to be."

Historically, Jha says, the medical and educational communities haven't cooperated well enough to assimilate new knowledge into everyday school agendas. He believes that helps to explain why public awareness of a problem like concussions is so uneven.

"The real issue here is that we need to go to the grassroots level," Jha says. "We're all working on the same issues here, and we need to unite the policy makers, the medical professionals, the athletes, the parents, the coaches, and the children. We need to utilize the government not to legislate, but to use the infrastructure of the government to go into curriculums nationally, and teach safe play. We need to change the culture of sport without taking the fun out of sport. And that's the concern the NHL and NFL have—they believe ticket sales are going to go down if they remove a physical element, and they also see UFC selling out large venues in minutes. To a lot of people it's pure entertainment, but we also have a responsibility to protect the athletes who are providing that entertainment."

Jha envisions a day where every person inside every Canadian arena can recognize the signs and symptoms of a head injury and provide a type of community watch to ensure the injured receive medical attention as quickly as possible.

"If we bring concussion awareness at the grassroots level to children nationally," Jha said, "what's going to happen is that, when parents and coaches go through the training, then if we're in Moose Jaw, Saskatchewan, or Cole Harbour, Nova Scotia, watching a game, and a child sustains what could be a concussion on the ice yet returns four shifts later, everybody is going to stand up—the parents in the stands, the players, and coaches on the other team—and say why is he out there? That will be a sign we're doing the right thing for our kids."

● ● ●

But not all the damage suffered by professional hockey players is physical in nature. A great deal of their trauma is mental. Hockey fans sometimes look only at an NHLer's wildly-out-of-whack salary and decide that anyone who earns a six-or-seven-figure salary each year must be living on cloud nine.

If only the equation was that easy. But it's not. People forget how pro hockey players came to be pros in the first place: They leave home in their mid-teens and live with people they've never met before. They ride buses on trips that can last for hours on end. They're in the public spotlight and as a result find themselves unable to trust people. And they're subjected to cruel and vicious insults from fans in the stands during games. According to a veteran sports psychologist who worked with hundreds of NHLers during his career, the average fan can't comprehend the psychological pressures elite players struggle with regularly—pressures that are compounded by the threat that their careers could be ended in an eye's blink by some overzealous opponent.

"Every single day, whether it's in practice or a game, players are being judged and they have to perform," says Dr. Paul Dennis, former psychologist for the Toronto Maple Leafs for 20 years. "Losing games, suffering injuries, family concerns— all of that gets pushed aside in the name of the games being played. But players are just as susceptible to mental illness as any member of the population. We hold them to a different standard. We hold them in high regard. We think they're invincible, but they're not."

Dennis, now a professor of sports psychology at the University of Toronto and York University, is convinced hockey coaching and management types at all levels can improve the mental support provided to players.

"In amateur hockey and up to the professional level, we can do a better job of helping athletes cope with the stresses of performance situations," Dennis says. "It's incumbent upon these organizations to provide some life skills for these players. Let's say somebody's been playing for Edmonton in the NHL for six years and then they get traded to the [New York] Rangers. Well, just because the player is mature in age, that doesn't mean he'll know how to cope in those situations. Teams that assume the asset—what they call the player—is comfortable, or teams that think they know a player based on what other players are saying about them, are teams that are assuming too much."

Again, we're not implying that hockey hasn't made strides in understanding the psychological effects on its players—but Dennis and others feel there is further to go. For example, he has seen players battle depression and the feeling that they're inside an entertainment machine that has little regard for them as individuals.

"Some will view themselves as victims in all of this," Dennis says of NHLers. "The players will get the support from their team as long as they stay with the team, but as soon as they leave to play for another team, their former teammates will vilify them for doing the same things they did when both players were wearing the same uniform. That's really stressful, and players realize that."

Traditionally, a combination of pride and fear of being marked as weak has kept NHL players largely silent and unable to ask for help to deal with mental health problems.

"They're not proactive in asking for help because they can't be—it's not in their nature," Dennis says of the average player. "That's why they need mental health assistance, and to me, a player reaching out isn't a sign of weakness on his behalf. It's about players who've dealt with pressure and the pressure has made an impact on them in some regard. We should be commending players who step forward like that."

• • •

Unlike Georges Laraque, Jim Thomson didn't have the luxury of being a six-foot-three, 270-pound behemoth to cement his status as one of hockey's toughest competitors. Yet Thomson nonetheless used the enforcer role to carve out a seven-season NHL career that included a stretch as the teammate of Wayne Gretzky in Los Angeles. And he did a very good job of it, racking up 416 penalty minutes in 115 NHL games and 1,067 more penalty minutes in the minors.

"I fought differently because of my size," says Thomson, who was drafted 185th overall by the Washington Capitals in 1984. "I was only six-foot-one and 220 pounds. I studied hours and hours of tape. I studied everybody I fought and anybody who was a fighter, and I fought on technique. I wasn't a guy who could go toe-to-toe against Bob Probert or Stu Grimson, because I wouldn't have lasted long. I was a smart fighter. If you look at my fight tapes, there were a lot of good fights, but there were boring ones, too; I wasn't willing to trade punches with a [notorious NHL tough guy such as] Joey Kocur or a Tony Twist. Sorry. I lasted 10 years in pro hockey by using my head, not my brawn."

Moreover, he wasn't some smoke-from-the-nostrils oaf who had no other hockey skills; in two of his seven years in the American Hockey League, he scored 20 or more goals, including 25 for the Baltimore Skipjacks in 1988–89. But, raised in a tough Edmonton family, Thomson little considered it to be out of bounds when he was involved in a fight.

"I used to gouge eyes, and I used to bite," he says. "I got suspended for biting. There was some really stupid behavior on my part. And the thinking behind that came partly from my older brothers. They're former bikers, tough guys, and they made it clear to me that you've got to fight to intimidate and fight to win. But when I look at it now, and I watch what I did on TV with my three kids sitting beside me, it makes me sick.

I mean, I had my finger two inches into another player's eye socket. It was ridiculous."

Thomson ached to be more of a contributor than opportunity allowed, but he was ruthless in the protection of his own turf as a fighter.

"Doing what you needed to do to keep the job was part of the job," he says. "There was a young kid who came into Washington one year aiming to be the tough guy there. But so was I; I had my 40 fights in Binghamton [of the AHL] the year before, and this kid came in challenging me for the job. I was so determined to not allow him to be an influence on [then–Capitals director of player development] Jack Button and [then-GM] David Poile, I fought him three times in camp.

"When I didn't get what I wanted to get out of the result of the fights, I tried to spear the kid in the throat. Thankfully I missed him—hit him in the chest—but Jack Button saw that and threatened to buy me out and sue me. 'Who do you think you are to do that?' I remember him saying. But all I was trying to do was show David Poile and Jack that I wanted this job. Anything to get the damn job."

Eventually, after a stint with the Hartford Whalers didn't work out for him and he passed through New Jersey and the Devils farm team in Utica, Thomson found a home in Los Angeles with the Kings during the 1990–91 season. The following year, he played a career-best 45 games—and had 162 penalty minutes. Yet even when he finally was a full-time part of an NHL team, the dream didn't feel fully realized.

"In the NHL, I was fourth-line only and got the tap to go over the boards and play when [an enforcer such as Detroit's]

Dave Brown was on the ice," Thomson says. "I begged for more time. I sat there and looked at guys like [former Kings teammate] Tony Granato and said, even though I'm in the NHL, the things I would do to get on the third line so I don't have to fight all the time."

That unease, combined with the inherent stresses of the enforcer role, drove Thomson headlong into the party scene. He boozed it up with the booziest of them and indulged in almost every drug you can name—including cocaine and pharmaceutical drugs such as the strong painkiller oxycodone (a drug known as "hillbilly heroin" for its easy access and widespread abuse by people from all walks of life). As noted earlier, oxycodone is what killed Derek Boogaard. And while many are reticent to tie Boogaard's death at age 28 to the job he did, Thomson doesn't doubt the pressures of the job funneled the young man toward a reckless lifestyle that contributed to his tragic demise.

"I've been around enough guys like this who are messed up on drugs and/or alcohol to know that it's solely because of the role they played," Thomson says. "There's no doubt in my mind. What bothers me is when people say hockey doesn't have a drug problem. That's absolutely untrue, and that's a message I want everybody to hear. They do have serious problems going on."

Thomson understands why Boogaard turned to oxycodone (also known by its brand name of oxycontin), and why enforcers such as the late Bob Probert (who was arrested in 1989 at the U.S./Canadian border for cocaine possession) and the late John Kordic—who died in 1992 at age 27 during a drug-fueled brawl with Quebec police—become entangled in a sticky shawl of self-medicating.

Hockey isn't the only place you see such self-punishing behavior. Thousands of soldiers fighting wars around the world have anesthetized themselves to be able to cope with the trauma. Although the scope of the fight is obviously far different in the hockey business, clearly, the combatants behave in much the same way.

"Oxycontin is a great stone, first of all, and it gets the job done in killing the pain," Thomson says. "Cocaine, marijuana, that's just part of the gig. One's an upper for you, and one is a downer. If you're coming off speed, you take something to help you go to bed. It's a vicious cycle."

The glorification of the enforcer role leads some to imagine that fighters are never happier than when they're trading clenched fists with another player. But Thomson says the opposite is true: that the lead-up to a fight—from the days and hours before right through each punch that's thrown—is terribly stressful on regular participants, and that the moment the fight stops is when the enforcer is happiest.

"When the fight was over, I was on cloud nine, because the anxiety of staying up all night, drinking and drugging to kill the fear of fighting, all that was over," he says. "I once saw Tie Domi say, 'I love to fight' when he was still playing, but you don't hear him saying that today, do you? You find one guy who says he loves to fight, and I'll say he's a liar. Nobody loves to fight. The fear of being knocked out and embarrassed? Nobody likes that."

But NHL enforcers don't just endure stress over their opponents from opposing teams. Sometimes, in the heat of practice or during training camps where jobs are being decided, they endure stress from members of their own team.

"What people don't understand was that not only did you have to fight in games, you'd also have to fight in practice occasionally," he says. "Keith Primeau and Bob Probert fought each other in practice. You could drop the gloves any day. I was in a half-dozen fights with my own teammates, just because of tempers."

For fighters like Thomson, there was no escape and no protection from the pressure to throw down. Even when he had previous experience with a player as a teammate, even when he liked a guy he once played with, Thomson didn't hesitate to go after him and try knocking him senseless.

"You're totally on your own in the league." Thomson says. "I went from L.A. to Ottawa in the '92 expansion draft, and by Christmas I was traded back to L.A. So my second game back in L.A., we play Ottawa. And my good buddy [as well as former Sens teammate and fellow enforcer] Darcy Loewen, who is a tough kid, is still on that team. So I go after him and we get it on. Looking back at it, we didn't need to do what we did, but in my mind at the time, I thought there was no better way to make an impression during my second go-around in L.A. than to mix it up with him.

"After the game was over, I thought to myself, there was no need for that. But the pressure convinces you that you need. to do it."

Soon enough—and with the illicit drugs establishing roots in his system—it didn't matter where Thomson went. He couldn't hide anywhere to escape the pressure, the fear in his mind that another fight, and the potential for disaster at every turn, would soon be at hand.

"When each season ended, I would go out to my cottage in Edmonton, where I'm from," he says. "And I was a guy who took my training very seriously. Knowing there could be five guys who wanted to take my job away from me the next season, I wanted to make sure I was the strongest. So I worked out every day, and skated five days a week. Really took care of myself. But at the same time, five nights a week, I had to get a buzz on, because of the fear of September coming and knowing I was going to have to fight as soon as training camp started and protect my job. That hovered over me, even during my summer holidays when I was supposed to be relaxing. You're sitting at your cottage asking yourself, 'How fun is this?' You just couldn't escape that anxiety, whether you were playing or not."

Thomson played his final NHL game in the 1993–94 season, but it wasn't until 2008 that he found a way out of his addictions and began to live a clean and sober life. A frequent panel guest with me on TSN's *Off The Record*, he initially always defended the need for fighting and enforcers in the game, but Probert's sudden death (and the postmortem report of his severe brain damage) in July 2010 alerted Thomson to the dangers enforcers subject themselves to every day they're on the job.

Very quietly, he had a revelation. He bravely began speaking out regarding the headshot issue and became one of the first former enforcers—if not, the first—to openly promote the banning of fighting altogether.

"I got to meet and know Bob Probert for five months when we worked together on [the 2008 Mike Myers hockey movie] *Love Guru*," says Thomson, who has founded a nonprofit charitable organization named Jim Thomson's Dreams Do Come True (www.jimthomsonsdreams.com) and works as a life coach and motivational speaker for young people. "My kids got to know Bobby really well during that time and thought he was just the greatest guy. We would sit and watch fights, and watch Bobby or me fight. Bob was, in my mind, the toughest guy to ever play, so I bragged him up that way to my kids. Then we talked about things after Bob died and the news about his brain study came out. My 14-year-old son, James, said, 'Dad, what's the future going to be for you?' I said, 'James, that's a great question, and I'm not naive enough to sit here and tell you that I'm going to be in great shape right up until the day I die. But it's a serious thing and we're going to do our best to deal with it.'"

As a former fighter now advocating a fight ban, Thomson has been heavily criticized for speaking out against the mushrooming problem of hockey violence. People have called him a hypocrite. But is there not something to be said for an honest change of heart? Where do people get off telling Thomson that, having survived a fighter's existence, he has to be a devoted slave to the pro-fighting mentality?

"The more I thought about it after Bob died, the more I thought, 'Why do we need bare-knuckle fighting in this sport?'" Thomson says. "And I came to the honest conclusion that we don't need it. The game is better off without it. With what we know about head injuries now, we don't need to have players having seizures or dying on the ice. Enough is enough."

If it was true fighting helped pave Thomson's way to the NHL, it was also true that it paved the way to at least a half-dozen concussions, substance abuse woes, and a looming sense he was well on his way to an early grave.

"I was going to die," Thomson says of knowing when he had hit rock bottom. "One night I had my three children sleeping around me and my heart was beating out of my chest. I knew I was in trouble. So I went to the NHL [-sponsored] rehab and learned how to deal with the depression of getting out of hockey. I never realized I had depression, but I did.

"With the help of the program, I had to educate myself on how to live a clean life, and since then, it's been three great years of sobriety. I'm up at five-thirty in the morning now, working out and living life clear and clean. I never knew what playing straight was all about."

Thomson's eldest son aspires to follow in his father's footsteps and build himself a career as a pro hockey player one day. But knowing what he knows now about the price that a fighter winds up paying, Thomson would never allow his own flesh and blood to pursue the role that he once played.

"He's a big kid, a defenseman, and he wants to learn how to fight and protect himself when he's playing the game," Thomson says of his son. "That's alright. But I told him that the enforcer role was not going to be his gig in life. If you make the game as a good defenseman, that's one thing. But following in my footsteps? No, that isn't going to happen."

CRITICAL MASS

WHEN HOCKEY BRUTALITY COLLIDES WITH POLITICS AND THE LAW

By and large, the hockey community fancies itself as immune from contact with outside authority, agencies, and organizations.

However, the NHL and other professional North American leagues have had frequent run-ins with the law and political forces. The reason isn't because of steroids, as was the case during the 2005 U.S. congressional investigation of performance-enhancing drugs in Major League Baseball. Instead, it has always been over-the-top incidents of aggression that have landed hockey in hot water with public authorities.

The clashes continue to this day. In fact, a currently unresolved case threatens to hold open the NHL's corporate eyelids à la *A Clockwork Orange* and force the league into drastically changing its attitudes toward fighting and a culture of revenge and retribution.

That lawsuit was filed in 2006 by former Colorado Avalanche forward Steve Moore, who was attacked by then-Canucks winger Todd Bertuzzi in a 2004 game in Vancouver.

Initially, Moore—who was knocked unconscious from behind by Bertuzzi and had his neck broken as well as a severe concussion in the multi-player pile-on that took place immediately after the punch—sat back and watched as the Province of British Columbia (B.C.) charged Bertuzzi with assault. Bertuzzi faced up to 18 months in prison if convicted, but bargained his way to a guilty plea in return for a sentence of probation and community service.

The outcome must have stiffened the resolve of Moore and his family—a smart, proud clan that included his brothers Mark (a former draft pick of the Montreal Canadiens) and Domenic (the youngest of the three, who would go on to play more than six seasons for various NHL teams)—to continue their fight against an aspect of the game that took Steve's career and passion away from him.

Two years after the incident, Steve Moore sued Bertuzzi and Orca Bay Ltd. (the former owners of the Canucks) in an Ontario court for $38 million in damages. As the defendants ran for cover, the legal motions flew: Bertuzzi [in turn] sued Marc Crawford, his former coach with Vancouver when he hit Moore, and Orca Bay's attorneys have made motions to distance their client from Bertuzzi. (Bertuzzi attempted to have Crawford included in Moore's lawsuit on the grounds he was following his coach's orders in targeting Moore; Crawford denied any insinuation or accusation he wanted Moore targeted at all.)

And while the NHL isn't involved in the lawsuit in a technical sense, a victory for Moore would almost certainly push the league to change policies regarding fighting and its retribution/revenge culture. A verdict against Bertuzzi and the Canucks would be based on the legal notion of "vicarious liability"—a term for imposing blame on an employer for the actions of an employee. A court would have to accept that the employer (Orca Bay) was in part responsible for its employee (Bertuzzi) and for not going far enough to stop him from attacking Moore.

But in doing so, the court could give the NHL no choice but to reverse course on its views about fighting and casual violence. If Moore can establish he did not consent to the type of assault Bertuzzi perpetrated on him, the league will have no wiggle room in enforcing its rulebook.

In addition, a massive financial payday from Bertuzzi and Orca Bay to Moore will have an immediate chill effect on fighting and over-aggressive play. What NHLer would dare engage in fisticuffs, knowing that he could be bankrupted by legal action for an injury suffered by his opponent? What coach wouldn't go out of his way to keep players in line for fear that he could be hauled into a courtroom one day and made to pay exorbitant attorney fees because of an awful choice from one of his charges?

Those are all questions that worry the NHL's most powerful men who prefer to see a game that includes fighting. A victory for Moore, a death on the ice, or a late-life lawsuit from a former player suffering from long-term concussion symptoms would trigger a series of events that would result in the power being taken away from them and placed in the hands of people who would agree to act more responsibly for the treatment and protection given to players and their families—judges, politicians, and hockey people willing to abide by more progressive regulations.

Unfortunately, many hockey administrators, management figures, and players feel those who know the game best should be the only ones permitted to pass ultimate judgment on the actions taken at the sport's highest levels; if some nosy lawyer or publicity-obsessed politician gets in the hockey world's way, it has never been reluctant to lash out in return. But, as society's tolerance for reckless behavior has lessened, hockey people have become more delicate in the way they talk about the law's relationship with the game.

As noted in Chapter 2, NHL president Clarence Campbell once was openly contemptuous of the league after a quartet of Philadelphia players were charged criminally by Ontario Attorney General Roy McMurtry in 1976. Campbell's confidence that the province and its institutions were all but feckless was well placed; as someone who had grown up inside the game, he was around when prosecutors and government representatives attempted to impose legal constraints on the NHL's product and failed miserably. He knew the courts viewed organizations like his as voluntary and private, and thus could afford to speak publicly to the league as a parent would to a child.

However, for the good student of history that Campbell was, he could not envision hockey's days to come. He could not have predicted the growing dismay many hockey lovers feel for the sport. He couldn't have foreseen advances in science and medicine that would paint a clearer, more troubling picture of the price paid by hockey players just for doing what a league perceives to be their jobs.

The arrogance with which Campbell treated the law no longer exists at NHL headquarters. Current commissioner Gary Bettman never would taunt legal authorities the way

Campbell did. He knows times have changed and the average hockey fan's appetite for destruction has been curbed significantly. He also knows that an increasing number of NHL team owners, including all-time great Mario Lemieux and the owners of the Montreal Canadiens and Ottawa Senators, have made clear their concerns over the sport's direction.

To top it off, Bettman's league is dealing with a massive lawsuit by a former player that could shake its policy pillars to their foundation. That's the real reason why NHL officials are so fearful behind the scenes about a potential legal challenge. Bettman is fully cognizant of the fact that, as powerful as he is, his power only extends so far. He knows there are other people out there with the capacity to push him in directions his owners don't want him to go.

The commissioner, who was a lawyer before he joined the NHL in 1993, has every reason to walk softly and hope nobody notices his league's big, bloodied stick. He and all lawyers know the courts can be fickle at the best of times. And all it would take is one court decision to force professional hockey to conduct itself much differently than it does today.

When we talk about the dangers of hockey violence and the reactions of the legal community to egregious on-ice incidents, we have to remember that the law has had to step in to police the sport's more outrageous incidents for more than a century. Even prior to the NHL's founding in 1917, people were severely injured—or worse—during hockey games.

The 2006 CBC hockey documentary *Hockey: A People's History* reported that four players were killed in 1904, while two more died in the following three years. One of those men was named Alcide Laurin, a young player from Alexandria, Ont. (just southeast of Ottawa), whose team was taking on opponents from nearby Maxville, Ont. on February 24, 1905. In the midst of a brawl, the 19-year-old Laurin was pronounced dead on the ice after he was punched in the chin and hit on the temple by the stick of notoriously vicious Maxville player Allan Loney.

In the aftermath of Alcide Laurin's death, the 24-year-old Allan Loney was charged with murder. The case was characterized by the elements of language—Loney was anglophone, as was the city of Maxville, while Laurin and the Alexandria area were stout French-Canadian Catholics. A little more than a month later—and with the charges reduced to manslaughter—Loney's trial was held. Numerous defense witnesses testified Loney's actions were instinctual and for the purposes of self-defense. And the prosecution had no answer for it, so on March 29, following some five hours of deliberation, the jury in the case acquitted Loney, no appeal was filed, and the charges were dropped.

Two years later, during a game in the Federal Amateur Hockey League (based between Eastern Ontario and Western Quebec), Cornwall player (and the league's leading scorer) Owen McCourt was killed in a brawl during a game against the Ottawa Victorias. Manslaughter charges for McCourt's death were laid against Victorias player Charles Masson. But in the subsequent trial, Masson was found not guilty, chiefly because the prosecution could not prove which blow killed McCourt.

Essentially, that was the pattern that repeated itself when hockey and the law collided for the next 90 years. A player would commit an especially awful act, a prosecutor would react to it with charges, and without the full participation of the hockey community, the charges would disintegrate in the initial stages of the legal system.

In Chapter 2, we referenced some other pro hockey incidents that resulted in legal charges. One, in the now-defunct World Hockey Association, saw Calgary Cowboys goon Rick Jodzio charged by Quebec authorities with assault for fighting Nordiques star forward Marc Tardif in 1976; Jozdio was one of the few players to plead guilty to the charges, but was fined just $3,000.

Two others took place in the NHL: Red Wings forward Dan Maloney was charged in 1975 in Toronto for attacking Leafs defenseman Brian Glennie, and performed a small amount of community service to remove the assault charge from his record.

As well, in 1976, four Flyers were charged in Toronto for their actions during a game against the Leafs. Two Flyers (Joe Watson and Bob Kelly) pleaded guilty to charges of common assault and assault causing bodily harm, respectively, and were fined; the other two Flyers (Mel Bridgman and Don Saleski) had their charges (assault causing bodily harm and common assault, respectively) dropped by the province.

"It's our view that in the last few years the word was out that somebody could make the big leagues by being a goon-type player," says former Ontario Attorney General Roy McMurtry, a driving force behind the prosecution of players at the time.

That said, serious jail time was never handed out in any of those cases, never enough of a real message delivered across the bow of a hockey establishment that showed no inclination toward making its players adhere to responsible levels of sportsmanship and proper decorum. The hockey world and the world outside it weren't yet ready for a thorough change in philosophy on hockey violence.

• • •

That's not to say those were the only instances when hockey players were charged for something they did during a game. In fact, professional hockey players facing legal repercussions has been a relatively consistent occurrence.

The infamous Ted Green/Wayne Maki stick-swinging incident in September 1969—that led to a fractured skull for Green and both players being charged (Maki with assault causing bodily harm, and Green with common assault)—ended with both players being acquitted.

In 1975, Boston Bruins forward Dave Forbes became the first pro athlete to be indicted for an alleged crime committed on the field of play. He engaged in a fight with Minnesota North Stars forward Henry Boucha and was knocked to the ice; after both men left the penalty box for serving fighting penalties, Forbes skated directly to Boucha and hit him in the eye with the butt end of his stick.

Boucha was cut by Forbes' stick—requiring 30 stitches—and had a bone near his eye cracked. As he put his hand over the eye to stop the flow of blood, Forbes then punched Boucha several times in the back of the head. Boucha was never the same player after the incident and retired two years later. After the incident, the state of Minnesota charged Forbes with aggravated assault, but the subsequent trial ended in a hung jury.

And you couldn't accuse the courts of only charging visiting teams with crimes against the home team. In October 1976, Dave "Tiger" Williams—one of the most beloved players in Toronto Maple Leafs history—was charged with assault causing bodily harm and possession of a dangerous weapon for attacking rugged Pittsburgh Penguins defenseman Dennis Owchar with his stick during a game in Toronto. Yet again, the charges fizzled, and Williams would be acquitted.

It wouldn't take long for another hockey case to appear on a court docket. In January 1981, NHL star Dino Ciccarelli was playing for the North Stars and was in Toronto when he struck Maple Leafs defenseman Luke Richardson twice in the helmet with his stick and punched him in the mouth.

Immediately after the game, Ciccarelli was charged with assault. And though the usual protestations were heard, in this particular case, the reactions of the usual parties involved began to change. Although Ontario judge Sidney Harris sentenced Ciccarelli to only one day in jail and gave him a $1,000 fine, Ciccarelli became the first NHL player to receive a jail term for an on-ice act. And Harris' tone in his ruling suggested that the world outside the realm of hockey was changing in the way it saw the NHL and what it allowed as part of the game.

"It is time now that a message go out from the courts that violence in a hockey game or in any other circumstances is not acceptable in our society," Harris said. He did not deny hockey was a physical, fast game, but ruled Ciccarelli had used more than an acceptable amount of force. Harris also warned that continued perpetrators of on-ice violence could, if the sport did not change its ways, "expect punitive measures, including jail sentences."

Another reaction to this incident also signaled the early tremors of change. John Ziegler, the NHL's president at the time Ciccarelli was charged, did not take the same arrogant approach toward the law as predecessor Clarence Campbell.

After Harris' ruling and sentencing of Ciccarelli, Ziegler wasn't irate in the least. "Although we are disappointed in the outcome of the case," Ziegler said, "it has been our belief that sports are not above the law."

• • •

Even amateur hockey players have found themselves targeted by the law—and with very good reason.

In April 1998, during an Ontario Hockey League game between the home team Plymouth (Michigan) Whalers and Guelph Storm, six-foot-two Plymouth enforcer Jesse Boulerice swung his stick directly into the face of skilled Guelph forward Andrew Long. At the time, *Sports Illustrated* writer Jeff MacGregor described what happened next:

"When Jesse swung his stick, he produced immediate consequences for Andrew," MacGregor wrote. "[A] broken nose, multiple facial fractures, a Grade III concussion accompanied by seizure, a contusion of the brain, two black eyes and a gash in his upper lip the size of a handlebar mustache. Had the stick landed a hand's width higher or lower, Andrew might have been killed."

Long needed 20 stitches for his injury, had his nasal cavity crushed, and had a blood spot on his brain. Boulerice was suspended for one year by the OHL, but played again the next season in the professional American League sitting out only 15 games.

Michigan authorities charged Boulerice with "assault to do great bodily harm less than murder." But following the pattern of other players charged in the past, he later pleaded no contest to a reduced charge (of aggravated assault) and was sentenced to just 90 days probation. Long was dismayed by the relatively light sentence Boulerice received from both the hockey and legal communities.

"I wanted him suspended for life," Long told the *Ottawa Citizen* in 2007. "People said, 'Don't you want him to go to jail? Don't you want to sue?' I said, 'No.' It is a hockey incident, but it's the worst kind of hockey incident. So what do you do? You give the worst penalty. And what's the worst penalty? A life suspension."

Long understood how close he was to losing everything—and in a sense, he did: he tried playing again after the incident, but couldn't continue at an elite level. That made him all the more incredulous and angry at Boulerice's quick return to the ice.

"I almost died," says Long, who didn't see Boulerice swing his stick and hit him before contact was made. "It was within a couple of inches either way of happening. If I would have seen him, my natural reaction would have been to tip my head back, and if I did that and he hit me in the neck, I would have been dead on impact. If it was two inches higher and I died, what [kind of suspension] would he have got then?"

Ten years later, the son of a legendary NHLer also felt the sting of the law. In March 2008, a brawl broke out during a Quebec Major Junior Hockey League (QMJHL) game between the Chicoutimi Sagueneens and the Quebec Remparts—a team owned and coached by Hall-of-Fame goalie Patrick Roy—and Roy's son Jonathan (a goalie for the Remparts) charged down the ice at Chicoutimi netminder Bobby Nadeau.

Nadeau made numerous indications that he did not want to fight Jonathan Roy, but Roy ignored them, knocked Nadeau to the ice, and proceeded to pummel his prone opponent mercilessly. The QMJHL investigated and suspended Jonathan seven games and fined him $500, while suspending Patrick Roy five games and fining him $4,000.

But that wasn't enough for an alarmed Quebec public. The province's ministry of public safety launched an investigation into the incident—and in July 2008, Jonathan Roy was charged by Saguenay courts with assault. In October 2009, he pleaded guilty to the allegation in court in exchange for an absolute discharge.

That slap on the wrist may be part of the reason why on-ice assaults (and charges) continued. In January 2010, during another QMJHL game, Rouyn-Noranda Huskies forward (and former captain of Canada's world junior hockey championship team) Patrice Cormier blindsided Remparts player Mikael Tam with an elbow to the head that sent Tam into convulsions on the ice.

The QMJHL reacted harshly, suspending Cormier for the remainder of the season and playoffs, but again the Quebec judicial system inserted itself into the equation, charging Cormier with assault causing injury. The charge still was making its way through the courts at the time this book went to press, but the incident showed that the clash between hockey culture and societal structure isn't at all likely to decrease.

• • •

Okay, let's say for argument's sake that the NHL continues to avoid having its players criminally prosecuted for their competitive lapses in judgment. A civil court ruling could, regardless, force the league to change course. This first became evident decades ago. In December 1990, former NHL tough guy Tony Twist was playing for the St. Louis Blues' American League affiliate in Peoria, Ill. During a game against the Milwaukee Admirals, he brutally checked Admirals goalie

Steve McKichan from behind into the boards, knocking him unconscious and causing a neck injury that would end his career that season at age 23. McKichan sued Twist and the Blues for his injury, and was initially awarded $175,000 by an Illinois jury. However, an appeals court quashed the verdict, reasoning that a severe body check like the one Twist applied was an acceptable part of pro hockey.

That case didn't push hockey into needed action, but again, one jury's ruling today could be another jury's rejected idea tomorrow. Indeed, despite the league's protestations to the contrary, for decades it has feared the law. During the flare-up of violence in 1975 and 1976, when Ontario Attorney General Roy McMurtry was frequently charging NHL players with assault (referenced earlier), insiders say there was a serious movement inside the league to scale back the acceptable limits of player aggression in response.

"Through government involvement and the law stepping in, that moved the NHL during that brawling period," says former league referee Kerry Fraser. "That really got their attention. Public opinion does have an effect. Yes, Gary Bettman has exhibited some arrogance, but reality eventually sets in. When [former NHL goalie and Canadian politician] Ken Dryden speaks out and says the culture of hitting has to change, the headline in *The Globe and Mail* said, 'Campbell says "butt out."'' So Colin Campbell basically said we don't tell you how to run the government, Ken, so you don't tell us how to run our game. That's the arrogance. And consequently, public opinion killed them."

Public sentiment isn't the only challenge for the league. Although Moore didn't sue the NHL specifically, a lawsuit directly targeting the league itself is not some far-fetched notion.

"One day, there will be, I'm sure, a lawsuit against the league itself," Toronto-based lawyer and professor Gord Kirke told *The Hockey News* in 2007. "Part of it is because of the increasing violence in the game, but part of it, too, is that there appears to be less of a collegial, mutual respect among players."

Kirke—a well-known and respected figure in the hockey community who has represented, among other NHLers, the retired Eric Lindros and still-active Blue Jackets star Rick Nash—believes the lack of respect players have for each other on the ice carries over off the ice.

"If you believe people are out to hurt people [on the ice] now, you have less respect for them and are therefore less hesitant to launch a lawsuit against them," Kirke says. "For a long time, players believed other players had a right to earn a living playing hockey and there used to be an unwritten code of honor that you wouldn't take anything out in court and kept matters within the game. But because the game has changed to a large extent and there's a lot more violence and risk of injury . . . now it's more a case of everybody for themselves."

In addition, Kirke says, there's a possibility the NHL Players' Association could be sued by a player accusing the union of not going far enough to protect its constituents.

"It's not just about what the National Hockey League may or may not want to do (in regard to rules and enforcement)," he says. "It's what they're able to collectively bargain with the Players' Association, as well.

"The players have, in the past, sometimes resisted things perhaps you think they would embrace—safety elements like helmets or full-face visors. You can see an argument being made, for example, if someone suffered a head injury that could've been prevented if full visors were mandated. You could see an argument being advanced that there was negligence on the part of the National Hockey League and the Players' Association, because they knew the proper thing would be to [mandate] a full visor, for example, but they wouldn't take that step, and left [a player] exposed [to injury]."

Allan Walsh, a longtime NHL player agent and former deputy district attorney in Los Angeles, has become one of the league's harshest and most vocal critics of its player protection measures. He has little faith that the league's current admin- istration truly intends to be proactive in pursuing a safer workplace for its players.

"The reality is, the league is only going to do as much as they feel they need to do to avoid widespread criticism from the public and the press," Walsh says. "And the only reason why the league is doing this is that they've become scared to death a player is going to die on the ice. The league is so worried about a death and that is because they're so afraid of government oversight or intervention into their private busi- ness. But the public and the media can make a very strong argument that, if the NHL isn't willing to police itself and pass what everyone considers to be fair and reasonable rules to stamp out this behavior, then the government ought to."

● ● ●

What happens when an NHLer or pro player does die on the ice due to a preventable situation? In 2009, the hockey world saw a player lose his life when—at the end of a fight—Ontario senior league player Don Sanderson died after his head struck the ice. The 21-year-old's death sparked a massive outcry—and his father, Mike, bravely spoke out regarding the need to crack down on hockey fights at all levels of the game—but no new rules were legislated by any political body, nor was there a public inquiry into the conditions that led to his tragic passing.

If a more prominent player were to suffer the same awful fate as Sanderson, it's unlikely the professional game would shrug its collective shoulders. At the same time, some hockey industry types doubt that the death of a well-known player would trigger government intervention to change the NHL's stance on fighting and violence.

"I don't know if the government will eventually insert itself into the situation or whether reality will just hit home if a player dies on the ice," says Anton Thun, a veteran NHL player agent. "You have to think fans and media will be up in arms at that point, but I don't think the league could just ignore the sentiment and continue on as if nothing had happened."

Some have theorized a death at the NHL level would push insurance rates for players through the roof and force the league and NHLPA to alter its current stance. But Thun is also skeptical of that situation materializing.

"I don't know that the death of one player, as tragic as it would be, is going to have a significant impact on the insurance industry as far as covering players," Thun says. "For the most part, the insurance players wind up taking out is not life insurance. It's disability insurance. So the predominant issue is not whether somebody dies on the ice, it's whether his skills have been diminished to the point he can no longer pursue a professional career. There is life insurance coverage through the [NHL]PA, but would a player death have a significant impact on the rates? I doubt it."

Instead, Thun believes it's the increasing number of head injuries that could be the trigger for skyrocketing player insurance rates. "What ends up happening with players who are injured—whether it's a knee injury, elbow injury, shoulder injury, or a concussion—is that once you've sustained an injury and recovered from it, the willingness of insurance companies to insure you is dramatically lowered.

"So they will do one of two things: either they'll eliminate that element of coverage from the insurance policy and basically say that if you're concussed, you're not covered. Or they'll increase the premium significantly to cover off the risk they're taking."

Regardless of whether the league chooses to change proactively or have change thrust upon it, there is a growing movement for government intervention to protect players. For years, Glenn Thibeault—a Member of Canadian Federal Parliament; one-time play-by-play man for the OHL's North Bay Centennials; and past hockey player, coach, and referee—has found himself increasingly concerned with what he's seeing from hockey at all levels.

"When you sign up for a contact sport, you consent to some inherent risk and being hit," says Thibeault, a member of the New Democratic Party representing Sudbury, Ont. "But what you're not consenting to is assault. Some of the stuff we're seeing, it's assault. And what I'm talking about is taking out that kind of thing."

Thibeault, who has called for the formation of a Royal Commission to study the increase of violence in sports, thinks the NHL is best left to govern itself and its players. However, he has no doubts that the league and hockey in general must ask itself some tough questions regarding the place and acceptance of hyper-aggression in the game.

"I'm playing tennis and you do something I don't like and I hit you over the head with my racquet, it's assault," Thibeault says. "But if that happens in hockey, it's two minutes for high-sticking. When do we say enough is enough?"

Like many, Thibeault cannot understand why the NHL doesn't do more to ensure as many of its players as possible are in the lineup every night—if not for the competitive aspect of the league, then for the business aspect.

"Players are looked at as a commodity, so you'd want your commodity playing so you can put more bums in the seats," says Thibeault, who also believes NHLers are seen as role models by young players. "If we say it's okay for pro players to knock each other out with no repercussions, kids are going to emulate what they see every Saturday on *Hockey Night in Canada* or on TSN."

If the NHL is ever challenged in court, one of its biggest problems will be convincing people it could never have foreseen a situation in which a player suffered catastrophic injury. That's because such an argument hasn't an ounce of truth.

"I told the NHL four or five years ago there would be trouble, when two game misconducts that I called were rescinded by the league," Kerry Fraser says. "They were direct hits to the head, and they were called good hockey hits. I said, boys, four or five years down the road, you're going to have such an overwhelming outcry of public opinion against you, you won't be able to defend it. And bingo, here we are."

• • •

The NHL's entanglements with political and legal actors are bound to continue for as long as the league and its feeder leagues excuse away wanton violence as a key feature of their product. Prosecutors will continue to react to public anger over incidents that will be replayed time and again on their televisions. Those who have been injured will continue to speak out regarding the pathetic lack of discipline given to those who have injured them. And perhaps, one of these days, a judge or jury will decide that hockey has had enough chances to fix itself and requires help whether it asks for it or not.

If that turns out to be the case, the game's gatekeepers will have only themselves to blame for a stark injection of reality into the sport's system. They had every chance to be ahead of the curve and allow experienced and knowledgeable hockey people to shape the rules and regulations of the game without outside interference.

That they chose not to, that they decided to forego all-around safety for the pursuit of cheap and disposable thrills, will be the ugliest of epitaphs for their legacies.

THE UNORIGINAL 10
COMMON ARGUMENTS FROM HOCKEY'S GUARDIANS OF THE STATUS QUO, AND HOW TO EASILY DEBUNK THEM

8

For as long as there has been gratuitous hockey violence, there has been a debate between those who derive large amounts of pleasure from it and those who believe the game can survive and prosper without it. You rarely, if ever, see this debate on the CBC's Hockey Night in Canada *or any programs of the NHL's other broadcasting partners, but that doesn't mean people have tired of the topic. In fact, the issue is debated more often, and more passionately, than ever before.*

If you're in tune with that debate long enough, you soon recognize familiar arguments made by fans who love their fights. With due respect, their talking points are so predictable I can recite and refute them in my sleep. Some of those people will suggest I hate the sport and suggest that I instead focus my writing talents on figure skating, rhythmic gymnastics, or some other sport played by women. Other avowed defenders of fighting will say I want to ban fisticuffs altogether (as if that could be possible in any sport). Still others will accuse me of trying to take players' personal responsibility out of the game. None of that is true, but that doesn't stop Joe Tribalism or stubborn pro-fight media types from convincing themselves otherwise. I just wish they were a little more creative in their debate points.

After more than a decade of covering the sport, I've heard the same claptrap so often I have no problem formulating my response to those charges before they've been fully made. Bearing this in mind, here's my handy guide to stickhandling any debate with your average fan of fighting and/or bare-naked barbarism.

Pro-Fighting Argument No. 1:

If you don't like fighting, you don't like hockey. Go watch something else that's less of a man's sport.

The first thing to note here: you're probably debating someone who hasn't considered (or refuses to consider) that the game is played differently outside the professional North American sphere. If you tell a fan from Helsinki or Stockholm the North American way is the only way to play hockey, be prepared to hear you're mistaken.

The second element of this for-fighting argument is the emasculation of the anti-fighting proponent. If you're not being told to cover the women's game—which, by the way, *everybody* in Canada watches every four years during the Olympic Winter Games—your suggested destination is to cover knitting, or figure skating, or anything relating to a female. That not-so-subtle message is hammered home by the use of the term "man's sport." The main intent of it is to intimidate you into believing hockey is more vicious and physical than any other sport and thus deserves to allow its players to police themselves. To say hockey is more brutal than an NFL football game (in which players have been known to squeeze each other's testicles during scrums for the ball) or a rugby contest (that has been known to have its athletes commit similar acts during similar scrums) is to belittle those athletes and the toughness it takes to withstand a cheap shot and not retaliate.

Hockey players very much enjoy the image they've earned over the years: that of the most well-mannered and humble competitors in mainstream professional sports. Unfortunately, when they presume the basic behavior expectations we have for athletes don't apply to them, they come off as arrogant exceptionalists. And the worst part is, in their rush to (humbly) declare themselves the toughest hombres on the sporting plain, hockey players regularly turn down the same degree of medical care other professional athletes receive. For example, when athletes in the mixed martial arts/ultimate fighting championship suffer a concussion, they're ordered to sit out and not fight or train for 30 days. Right now, an NHLer could be concussed and return to the ice only 15 minutes later. And that's after the league "improved" its stance on headshots.

Reflect on that: a sport thought to be the most barbaric in the modern age does a better job of safeguarding its competitors than North American hockey.

Pro-Fighting Argument No. 2:

Nobody in the stands leaves the building in disgust or sits down in boredom during a fight. In other words, fans love it.

While it's not assured that reducing egregious violence in hockey would appeal to North American audiences, it's also not assured they would reject it and take their disposable incomes elsewhere. To this point, we've only tried it the violent way, so it might be nice to eventually prove—or disprove—the connection.

If that assertion were true, and games were played that didn't have fights in them, wouldn't there be mile-long line-ups of people requesting refunds? Wouldn't those refund lines stick out like a sore thumb during games that almost never feature fights, including playoff games and Olympic games? The truth is, we never see those things come to pass. People can watch a thrilling hockey game—where the main focus is on scoring more goals than the opposing team, not intimidating its members—without wondering where the fighting had to come into it.

In fact, more hockey fans—hard core and casual—tune in to fight-free hockey than NHL hockey. Consider, for example, the gold-medal game at the Vancouver 2010 Olympic Winter Games between the U.S. men's team and their Canadian rivals. That game was the most-watched hockey game on U.S. television since 1980, when the United States upset the heavily favored Soviet Union in the final matchup of the men's teams at the XIII Olympic Winter Games in Lake Placid, New York. Some 27.6 million Americans tuned in for the 2010 Olympic final—more than the Masters golf tournament (with 14.3 million viewers), the most-watched game from the 2009 World Series (22.8 million), auto racing's famous Daytona 500 (16 million), and college football's 2010 Rose Bowl (24 million). When the 2010 Olympic final went into overtime, the U.S. TV audience spiked—to a high of 34.8 million viewers.

Meanwhile, in Canada, the 2010 gold-medal hockey game was—not surprisingly—the most-watched sports TV show in the country's history. Twenty-six-and-a-half-million Canadians, nearly two-thirds of the country's population, watched at least part of the game.

Do you know how many fights took place in that game? Zero. Here's the breakdown of penalties in the game: there was a tripping penalty called in the first period, three more penalties called in the second (one each for high-sticking, interference, and tripping), and none called in the third period or overtime. Amazingly, the alleged "release valve"—fighting—didn't find its way into the game. No "message" needed to be sent by either team via a so-called policeman (of course, no enforcers ever make their country's national team, because fights aren't tolerated to the same degree as they are during regular-season games in North American leagues). No perceived cheap shot required retribution from either side. While the game was still physical, the main feature it used to captivate the game's fans was skill.

Yes, there's no denying hockey fans will stand and cheer when two opponents drop their gloves and engage in a punch-up. But what if you took an attractive young woman to center ice and had her perform a striptease for the crowd? I'd bet many in attendance would love that as well—even though a burlesque act has about as much to do with an average hockey match as a hockey fight. But a burlesque show would never fly with the NHL as it would cheapen the sport and distract from the real spectacle talented players can provide. Obviously, the league's policy makers cannot see how fighting leads directly to those same awful results. And any time the hockey establishment tries to take the high road—as

Gary Bettman attempted to do when suspending Sean Avery for making crude remarks about another player's girlfriend— the prevalence of fighting stops the NHL from taking it.

When your game permits and encourages its players to cede to their baser natures, it can't claim to be family-friendly when the mood strikes.

Pro-Fighting Argument No. 3:

You want to ban fighting, when even NHLers say they don't want fighting banned from the game.

Here's a different but also common and empty angle used by fight fans: the red-herring, patently false concept of "banning" fighting from hockey. In a recent poll of NHL players, that trick was used, with the expected result that 98 percent did not want fighting banned from the game.

I've never argued fighting should—or even could—be completely removed from hockey. You can no more make it disappear on the ice than from any team sport game. Baseball still has the occasional bench-clearing brawl and football will have a fistfight every now and then; for some, there's an unavoidable allure to settling matters on their own that no amount of education, or disciplinary action, will prevent.

You can't ban fighting. But you can increase the punishments for fighting to persuade players—by punitive and compounding financial measure, if need be—that they cannot habitually act in that way. You can hammer repeat offenders with punishments that will make them think twice about taking hockey justice into their own hands.

As Mario Lemieux suggested in a letter to the NHL, you also can fine organizations who employ boundary-breakers and ensure it's not only the players who are responsible for their actions. He proposed a system in which teams could be fined anywhere from $50,000 (for a player suspended for one or two games) to $1 million (for a suspension lasting 15 games or longer), with fines doubling for repeat offenders in the same season.

If you ask players if they want to ban fighting, we know what the answer will be. If you ask them if they want to rid the game of repeat-offender injury artists who exist neither to score goals nor to defend against them, the answer will be significantly different.

Indeed, when the NHLPA polled its membership in 2011 and asked players if they wanted to repeal the rule that heavily punishes the instigators of fights, 66 percent of respondents said they did not.

Pro-Fighting Argument No. 4:

Without fighting, the game won't be any safer. In fact, it will be more dangerous, because sticks will be used more often as weapons and players won't be able to make an opponent pay a price for dirty play.

This argument ignores NHL reality, a place where sticks are occasionally used as weapons and dirty players are allowed to continue being dirty players except for the most extreme cases. If the league were clean other than for the occasional fight, I would concede the point. But as we saw in Chapter 1, the NHL has gradually slipped into chaos—with near total deference to the pro-fighting mentality. And in the ultimate indictment of what little difference fighting is as a deterrent, the league's designated fighters are often the ones who take cheap shots.

Fighting exists, and the league still has Matt Cooke, Cal Clutterbuck, Sean Avery, Maxim Lapierre, and other players infamous for crossing the line of acceptable behavior. Fighting exists, and the league still has grievous and regular instances of thuggish acts and irresponsible play. As always, those who claim fighting is a deterrent simply choose to ignore, or are incapable of understanding, that meting out deterrence is the role and responsibility of the league, not the athletes who compete within the league.

Incredibly, longtime fighting advocate and former player/coach/GM Mike Milbury admitted as much in March 2011, on a Saturday-night broadcast of *Hockey Night in Canada*. Speaking during the second-intermission "Hot Stove" segment, Milbury shocked host Ron MacLean and journalists Pierre LeBrun and Eric Francis when he cited the shocking number of concussions that season (more than 10 percent of the league had suffered head injuries), questioned the need for goons, and then really let the hockey establishment have it.

"The only reason we have fighting in the game is because we like it," said Milbury.

This floored MacLean, a steady and public supporter of fighting in the game, who tried suggesting fisticuffs are necessary in that they help police the game.

"Don't tell me we police it, Ron," Milbury barked back. "It's still hogwash."

It's certainly hogwash on the U.S. collegiate hockey scene. In NCAA hockey, any players who choose to fight are automatically ejected from the rest of the game; in addition, players can incur longer suspensions if they are in more than one fight. Needless to say, goons such as Derek Boogaard and Colton Orr never played in the NCAA.

Any sports organization can stamp out any action it wants. In the NHL's case, if the league implemented stricter rules on fighting which led to players taking more liberties with their sticks, the subsequent solution would be to punish those stick infractions, not for league administrators to abdicate their duties as overseers of the sport under the guise of "tradition."·

Pro-Fighting Argument No. 5:

What are you so upset about? Nobody gets hurt in a hockey fight!

This hot, steaming slice of dogma has been swallowed whole— for decades—by fisticuffs fans. However, with the growth of players in height, weight, and strength, and with every additional medical report, it is being proven factually false.

Ask Todd Fedoruk if nobody gets hurt in a fight. The former NHL enforcer played 545 regular-season games, amassed 1,050 penalty minutes, and suffered a slew of horrendous injuries in his 10 years in the league.

In November 2003, Fedoruk was playing for the Philadelphia Flyers and took on Islanders goon Eric Cairns one night. At six-foot-two and 232 pounds, Fedoruk was a mound of muscle and not someone to take lightly—but against Cairns, a six-foot-six, 241-pound behemoth who put up 1,182 penalty minutes in just 457 NHL games, he was a mere mortal. Fedoruk actually availed himself well in the throw-down, but after Fedoruk's adrenaline dipped to normal levels, he discovered his orbital bone was broken by Cairns. He had it repaired and was back playing for Philadelphia just 24 days later.

In October 2006, Fedoruk (who had moved on to become a member of the Anaheim Ducks) took on Minnesota Wild fighter the late Derek Boogaard, arguably the toughest NHL enforcer in the last decade—and at six-foot-seven and 265 pounds, even more imposing than Cairns. Boogaard dropped Fedoruk to the ice with a thundering punch that shattered his cheekbone; Fedoruk would require serious reconstructive surgery that included titanium plates being permanently implanted into his face.

But he kept on playing and he kept on fighting, and in March 2007—yes, the same season he was pummeled by Boogaard—Fedoruk was knocked unconscious by New York Rangers goon Colton Orr and had to be carried off the ice on a stretcher.

Ask the families of Bob Probert and Reg Fleming—two fighters from two different NHL eras—if nobody gets hurt in a fight. Both Probert (who died unexpectedly in 2010 at age 45 after suffering a heart attack) and Fleming (who died in 2009 at age 73) were discovered to have the degenerative brain disorder known as chronic traumatic encephalopathy (CTE). As he was only in his mid-forties, Probert had not yet begun to display any CTE symptoms (including dementia symptoms such as confusion, depression, memory impairment, and aggression), although his widow said he did exhibit some mild symptoms such as short-term memory loss and a "short fuse."

Fleming, on the other hand, lived nearly three more decades than Probert; as such, his descent into dementia was more prolonged and public. He was a manic-depressive in his forties, drank excessively, and had more trouble controlling his temper after his playing days than he did while he was out on the ice.

Fleming and Probert represent the tip of the iceberg when it comes to the barrage of neurological afflictions many doctors fear they'll discover in retired NHL players. Fleming played most of his career prior to the Broad St. Bully days of the 1970s, and those players are now solidly inside their senior years. Fearing that the worst is ahead of us is only natural. In addition, the May 2011 death of Boogaard provides another example of designated fighters who buckle psychologically under the stress of the role.

Nobody gets hurt in a fight? That is a breathtaking lie. We're only scratching the surface of discovering exactly how much damage fisticuffs actually do.

Pro-Fighting Argument No. 6:

This is a media-created controversy. If you didn't write and/or talk about it, nobody would care!

I'm going to answer this one by starting with a question: Do you know who Steve Wilstein is? He's the former Associated Press reporter who covered major league baseball in the late 1990s, when the sport was enjoying renewed popularity based in large part on the home run race between St. Louis Cardinals slugger Mark McGwire and Chicago Cubs counterpart Sammy Sosa. Wilstein was at McGwire's locker in August 1998 when the label of a bottle of pills caught his eye. He wrote the name down on his notepad, asked McGwire questions about it, followed up with some research, and eventually wrote a story that would enrage many, but ultimately spoke truth to a sport that didn't want to listen.

Wilstein wrote about androstenedione—a steroid that increased testosterone levels in its users, and that was a performance-enhancing substance banned by the NFL, the International Olympic Committee, and U.S. college sports—and the baseball world reacted with fury. Not at itself, but at Wilstein.

McGwire lashed out, accusing Wilstein of "snooping" near his apparently sacred locker. Cardinals manager Tony LaRussa attempted to have the journalist banned from the team's locker room. Worst of all, other journalists ignored the story and turned their artillery on one of their own; when he wasn't being called "unprofessional" by other writers, he was accused of "inventing a scandal" and his work was being referred to as "tabloid-driven controversy."

Of course, the real controversy for baseball came seven years later, when the steroid issue mushroomed to the point another slugger (San Francisco Giants outfielder Barry Bonds) had a drastically bulked-up body and made mincemeat of the earlier home run record set by McGwire and Sosa. (Bonds hit 72 home runs in 2000—two years after McGwire had 70 and Sosa, 66. This, after the previous record of 61 homers in a single season had stood for 37 years before McGwire and Sosa broke it.) By then, U.S. politicians got involved, commissioning official congressional hearings in 2005. It was an act many saw as political grandstanding, but baseball had nobody but itself to blame; if it had put its house in order in the years leading up to the hearings, there would have been no public appetite for them.

Instead of listening to people like Steve Wilstein—who dared to question the chorus of the blind faithful—baseball carried on its business as usual, sullying the sport irreversibly and tearing down the idols (not to mention, the validity of player performance statistics during the steroid era) it specialized in creating before that period. In the same way its players did, major league baseball destroyed a vital part of itself because it was willing to sacrifice the integrity of athletic competition for the competitive advantage androstenedione and other steroids provided. Only the players were publicly shamed for making that choice, but the owners and commissioner Bud Selig were equally to blame. And the same pattern is being followed by hockey now—only the drug's name has changed.

Indeed, the parallels between baseball's denial of its steroid problem and hockey's denial of its addiction to over-the-top violence are eerily similar. Is that a media creation? Nobody would be happier than me for that to be true. The facts, however, are not in the hockey establishment's favor.

Pro-Fighting Argument No. 7:

Let's be honest and admit we like fights in hockey strictly on a visceral level. What's wrong with appealing to the ultimate fighting championship (UFC) demographic?

If there's one argument I'd accept from the pro-fighting crowd, it's that certain hockey fans enjoy watching two players pound one another because it satisfies a primal urge. I've felt it and cheered for it when I was a kid in the 1970s and wouldn't deny it can be a natural occurrence in a contact game.

But if owners of teams in other professional leagues recognized that element as a selling point that could grow their business, does it not follow they would have incorporated fighting into their sports? Why doesn't the NFL allow one roster spot on all teams to go to a player who can't otherwise compete at that elite level, but who's part of the club because he can clean the clock of virtually anyone? Why won't the NBA make room for muscle-bound monsters who can't jump over a half-thimble, but who are great at "sending messages" via hand-delivered concussions?

I'll tell you why: because those leagues have faith in their product and understand fans pay to watch sports stars thrive, not survive. Those leagues couldn't appeal to spectators, let alone kids and their families—not only as fans, but also in terms of recruitment and participation in amateur basketball—if they didn't take every measure possible to make those athletes as safe as possible. As you're seeing in examples throughout the book, the NHL has never taken that approach to its players.

As for the mixed martial arts angle: I'd counter that the massive profits being made by the UFC—Dana White, the organization's president, estimated the organization was worth US$2.5 billion in 2010—only strengthens my argument that the NHL should get out of the punching business.

The fact is, the NHL can't compete in that field anymore. When I was a kid, we had 20 TV channels, no video games, and the chance to watch boxing maybe once a week on ABC. If that didn't satiate your cravings for a good dust-up, hockey provided a nice alternative you could rely on to be there when you tuned in. Times have changed. Now a youngster can choose to watch or participate in video games, so-called "extreme sports," or the UFC, any time, day or night. Now it isn't so necessary to see two men punch each other while balancing on skates.

Indeed, if the NHL were to try and keep pace with mixed martial arts, they'd need to play more to the goons and give them more leeway to engage in fights. When the league already has team owners, players, and fans speaking out about the current level of chaos, that's not going to happen. So the NHL's smartest choice involves two parts: first, the league has to admit the UFC has made obsolete that aspect of North American hockey; and second, it must focus on NHLers' speed and skill that cannot be replicated by any other athletes, rather than the brute barbarism that is now found in abundance.

Nobody says they'll make that choice. But never let them say nobody proposed an alternative to their vision. Some people did, and they rejected it.

Pro-Fighting Argument No. 8:

It's all about the damned instigator rule. If the NHL would repeal it, we could protect elite players. Hell, even the players want the instigator rule removed!

This is simply and demonstrably wrong. As noted in the answer to the third argument in this section, two-thirds of players who responded to a 2010 NHLPA poll said they did not want the instigator rule repealed. (In addition to a 10-minute misconduct penalty, the instigator rule assigns an extra two-minute minor penalty to the player who starts a fight, making goons and their coaches reluctant to instantly drop the gloves.)

Therefore, when Wayne Gretzky told TSN broadcaster Michael Landsberg the following . . .

> *Let's try [repealing the instigator rule] for one year just to satisfy everybody's curiosity... [I]f we all think and*

everyone feels *[emphasis added] that [repealing] the insti-*
gator issue will change things, then let's try it for awhile.

. . . he was factually misinformed about "everyone" in the
NHL playing community believing the game will be better by
repealing the instigator rule. Some players feel that way, but
not a majority. Even the game's greatest player can be wrong,
and No. 99 clearly is in this instance.

Gretzky's comment aside, those who advocate for the
removal of the instigator rule have awful short memories. The
instigator rule was implemented in the 1992–93 NHL season
to try and curtail the number of nonsensical, late-game brawls,
and because goon-type players had been attempting to lure
star players into fights.

To say the NHL can be made safer by giving more behavioral leeway to a class of player who has demonstrated time
and again he cannot handle that responsibility is to say society
can be made safer by ensuring all citizens are armed with guns.
Neither is true. By flooding an environment with weapons, all
you do is increase the likelihood of more victims. Similarly,
providing more time, space, and leeway for hockey enforcers
only provides more opportunities for them to seriously hurt
someone, whether or not that someone "deserves" it.

Pro-Fighting Argument No. 9:

**You've never played the game. All elite-level play-
ers understand the need for fighting and violence in
hockey. Leave it to the experts!**

At its core, the I'm-better-than-you argument is intended
to protect hockey establishment members from being

confronted with the logical fallacies of their creeds and deeds, and to limit public discourse to establishment members and/ or sycophant stenographers masquerading as independent-minded journalists. This type of statement normally signals desperation on the part of the person making it. And it's not only employed by former NHLers; numerous other professional athletes fail to come to terms with the media and its functions, as do employees of political and governmental agencies, and many would prefer to blame the questioners than deal honestly with the questions. That's nothing new.

Taken to its logical extreme, that approach would mean only Wayne Gretzky and Mario Lemieux could comment on each other's games and legacies, only Patrick Roy could argue that sure-to-be-Hall-of-Famer Martin Brodeur bene-fited from a supremely talented New Jersey Devils defense and isn't as talented as the Canadiens/Avalanche legend was on the ice, only enforcers could praise or pan the actions of other enforcers.

Think of what the world would look like if we transferred that philosophy to other areas of public life. Would we think it wise if hard-news organizations farmed out their political coverage so politicians were scrutinized by fellow politicians?

Of course not. There's tangible value in an adversarial press. And just because athletes and administrators don't agree with being criticized and questioned does not reduce or elimi-nate that value.

Beyond that element, what about the players who don't accept the addiction to retribution that characterizes North America's version of the game? What about former NHLers such as Mike Bossy and Serge Savard, or Bobby Hull? What about young players such as David Perron, who openly speak out about the need to ban all hits to the head while there's still time to save budding careers—such as his own? What about top-level player agents such as Pat Brisson and Allan Walsh, who recognize the game cannot continue without cannibalizing the precious core of talent that drives it?

What about lifelong hockey men such as former Calgary Flames GM (and current TSN TV analyst) Craig Button? He is one of the more outspoken advocates for an immediate and aggressive campaign to rid the game of staged fights and other needless violence—does that mean he doesn't know the game, either?

"These are all workplace safety issues," says Button, whose late father, Jack, was a GM of the Pittsburgh Penguins and director of the NHL's Central Scouting Service before his tragic passing in 1996. "In a contact sport, there will be inadvertent contact to the head. It's a physical sport. But contact to the head, in light of what we know, physically and mentally? No. I see no good reason why we can't have a headshot ban."

Button doesn't buy any of the pro-fighting propaganda espoused by the hockey establishment.

"This premeditated fighting doesn't belong in the game," he said. "Go through all the coaches of the NHL and tell me how many of them were fighters. None of them were. And these guys are telling players to go and fight? I'm a proponent of eliminating fighting from the game. I don't think it belongs, I think it's stupid, and this idea that eliminating fighting will lead to more stickwork? Wrong. We just have to give more power to the officials and tell them that stickwork also has to be cracked down on. So I say get fighting out of the game. I have no time for it."

Button also doesn't believe in the notion of "finishing your check"—hockey code for the willingness to barrel into any opponent as quickly and viciously as possible.

"It's easy—if you don't have the puck, you're not allowed to be hit," Button says. "You can rub a player out with a hard check, but hitting a guy just to soften him up? Sorry. This isn't war. We want kids in the game—why would parents put their kids in hockey for that?"

Also a former assistant GM of the Stanley Cup–winning Dallas Stars, Button thinks the NHL isn't doing enough to change the culture of the game and disputes those who would say you can effect change in hockey by starting to change the grassroots levels first.

"You cannot lead from the bottom up," he says. "You lead from the top down, and the NHL has to be the leader in this."

That said, Button has no doubt that attitudes are changing rapidly and that the game is headed toward a more progressive end.

"What we're starting to see here is a groundswell," he says. "If we know what our endgame is, why aren't we getting there? And I know the endgame here—we're going to have a game with no fighting, by which I mean you'll be ejected from the game for a fight. We're going to have a game where there's no headshots allowed. Zero tolerance there. So if we know that's the end game, what the hell are we waiting for? NHL owners are bright people—but what?—are you going to hang on to the current rules for another year or two and have another Marc Savard on your hands? Is that what we want? No, so let's get past this and evolve already."

Why are the words of experienced, important people like Button not being heeded? Why aren't their suggestions taken with respect and appreciation? It is extremely outrageous that hockey has failed them on some level, and equally outrageous to consider the countless young people who have been turned off by the sport and have abandoned it for something with an acceptable amount of sophistication. It also is downright laughable anytime somebody tries to use the "you-haven't-played-the-game" routine. The argument ignores the fact that behavior exhibited by NHLers is mimicked by pro and amateur players in arenas across North America. The ripple effect is widespread and devastating.

And whether you've played the game at the professional level or not, you're allowed to observe that reality and comment on it to your heart's content.

Pro-Fighting Argument No. 10:

I guess you just hate hockey.

To be perfectly honest, none of the previous arguments make my blood boil anymore, but this one comes closer than all the rest put together. It is undiluted arrogance for the hockey establishment's power brokers to presume their idea of the game is inherently superior to anyone else's, and that those who disagree do so with malice in their hearts.

Nothing could be further from the truth. I criticize the game because I grew up on it, because it means something to me, because I believe it can be better. And no hockey lifer wearing a pair of institutionally provided blinders is going to convince me I don't have a right to comment on the game.

If I wanted to, I easily could turn such an accusation around and argue that those who advocate for fighting in hockey are the ones who hate the actual game and are compelled to "accessorize it" with the spectacle of two men punching each other repeatedly until one of them falls over. But I'm not willing to do that. I'd never try and extinguish the debate by claiming that my preferences for the game are the only ones of value. The opposite is true: I think there are many ways the game can be played, and that they all have inherent advantages and disadvantages.

So forgive me if I snort derisively when some intellectual lightweight tries to bully me into submission with this particular attack. All it proves is that the person saying it is bereft of any further arguments, and doesn't have anything to add to the conversation.

THE ENLIGHTENED

THE SPORT'S MOST PROGRESSIVE MINDS ON MAKING THE GAME SAFER

We've examined hockey's violence addiction throughout this book and presented arguments suggesting ways to change that for the better. And in my many years of covering the game for The Hockey News, *I've found there's no shortage of former and current players, coaches, agents, and others associated with the game who see the toll being taken on it and have their own ideas on how to make the sport more responsible in caring for its participants.*

Even as recently as five years ago, the majority of those people were reticent to speak up, for fear of losing potential job opportunities, or because of the inevitable backlash they would experience from those with a vested interest in keeping the game as is. But with the steady increase in over-the-top violent incidents, and with higher-profile victims whose permanent absence from the game could hurt the entire industry, that reluctance is changing, and changing quickly.

These days, more people are feeling compelled to make their views known. More people understand that public opinion is not headed back to the days when Broad St. Bully hockey was the preferred way the game should be played. What follows are extended discussions I've had with many of the game's brightest minds. They don't all agree on the causes of or the solutions to the game's problems, but they do all agree on one thing: maintaining the status quo is not an option.

• • •

Mathieu Schneider *was a standout NHL defenseman for 21 seasons, played in two All-Star Games, won the Stanley Cup with the Montreal Canadiens in 1993, and took on a leadership role in his later years as a player by serving on the NHL competition committee and as a player executive within the NHL Players' Association. After retiring in 2010, he became special assistant to NHLPA executive director Don Fehr.*

On the rise in concussions: It's certainly our top priority [at the NHLPA] right now. The concussion issue is the number one issue; players have to feel they can play and perform at 100 percent, and play and be safe out there. There are certainly legitimate concerns right now regarding the combination of rule changes coming out of the lockout, as well as the size and speed of the players, and the age of the players. There's been a perfect storm where nobody anticipated these events would happen, but now we have to try and figure out different ways to solve it.

On the best ways to address the growing problem: I don't think there's just one thing you can change. It's more a list of three or four things. Number one is the on-ice rules; number two is the supplementary discipline element; and number three would be equipment changes. Players feel invincible with shoulder pads and elbow pads being so big. When I came into the league, the pads were small enough that if you landed on your elbow or went into the boards hard, you felt it for a couple days. So the equipment, to me, could have a major impact.

But beyond that, there's number four: there needs to be a culture shift in addition to what's going on out there on the ice.

On the urgency for making the sport safer: As a guy who was a member of the [NHL] competition committee, we could always debate things until we're blue in the face. But this is something everyone feels a real sense of urgency about. These are life-altering decisions we're making, and when you see so many players being affected—not to mention the players who've had their careers ended early—there's blame to go around, but players have to realize it's not a knee injury and you can't just shake it off and keep playing through blurriness and dizziness.

With what we know about concussions and what we continue to find out, we need to do something sooner than later. There's definitely a lot of work that needs to be done over a short period of time, and we want to make the game as safe as possible as soon as possible.

On his own experiences suffering concussions as a player and watching teammates attempt to deal with the issue: In my career, I had maybe two concussions that I missed time for. And I had a bunch of smaller concussions before I started wearing a mouthpiece. But at the [2011 NHL]

All-Star Game meetings, we were told that 87 percent of players had at least three prior concussions before coming to the NHL. That, to me, says a lot. And I'm sure the real numbers are higher than that.

Because of concussions, I have friends that had trouble taking a shower a couple years after they retired [as the water pressure is simply too painful cascading down on their heads]. [Former Oilers and Kings enforcer] Marty McSorley just had a double-hip replacement, but there's no replacing a brain.

On the disturbing lack of player awareness during NHL games: [NHLPA executive] Rob Zamuner started to look into what it looks like in the [Ontario Hockey League], and one of the things that keeps coming up is that players on the ice aren't as aware as they used to be, especially in situations coming along the boards, or coming through the middle of the ice. When you think about it, we're coming into a generation of NHL players here that allowed no hitting on the ice until they were 10, 11, 12 years old. Now [those youth amateur leagues and national agencies] want to make it 13 or 14 years old.

But for example, I watched the hit [Minnesota agitator Cal] Clutterbuck took [in 2011 from New York Islanders enforcer] Trevor Gillies; on the hit that took place just before Gillies comes in and reactively hits Clutterbuck, Clutterbuck hits a Wild player who sees the puck in his feet, puts his head down and faces the boards. That would never happen in a million years and definitely not when I first started playing.

But you see the same problem now when players chase a puck down into the corner and face the boards to protect the puck. You would just never do that. I used to give it to [former Red Wings teammate] Dan Cleary all the time, and I don't even think he faced the boards to draw a penalty; I think he just did it.

I said, "You'll get killed one day, 'Clears'—even if you do draw a penalty, you're going to wind up in the hospital one day with a broken neck."

On the NHL's post-lockout emphasis on speed, and the way the game has changed because of it: I think there were unintended consequences of the rule changes coming out of the lockout. With the obstruction crackdown, guys are bigger, faster, and stronger and they're coming at you at full speed. I know there will be discussion on how to address that at GM meetings, but I think players need to be involved in those discussions.

The players that are on the ice today need to have input, because the game changes in different ways every year. If you haven't played post-lockout, you have no idea how much faster it is out there. It's like playoff speed, all year long.

On the role coaches ought to be playing in changing the NHL's culture of predatory hits: There's a responsibility for coaches to teach players how to be aware and be safe on the ice. And I know that's not going on. I know it's not. As long as coaches keep sending players out on the ice whose sole purpose is to run their opponents and to hit, I don't know you can change that mentality so much. A player like Trevor Gillies thinks he needs to play the way he does to stay in the league. And you can't just fault the player for thinking that way.

On the renewed focus on concussions brought about in 2011 by a serious head injury to Penguins superstar Sidney Crosby: Sometimes the fact it happens to a superstar player makes everything move along quicker and benefits everyone in the game. It's just a matter of time before it happens to more star players. With the speed and the size of the guys who play in this league, it's just inevitable.

On the need for the NHL to protect the star players of the game: The stars of the league are the guys who drive the game, who the people want to come out and pay to see. Are they going to sell fewer tickets if Pittsburgh comes out to L.A. and Sidney Crosby and Evgeni Malkin aren't playing? Absolutely, they're not going to sell as many tickets. We want to see the guys on the ice, we want to see a safe game, and we want to see their skills come out every night.

• • •

Murray Costello *played four years in the NHL and went on to become president of the Canadian Amateur Hockey Association (now Hockey Canada) from 1979–98. He has been prominent in the building of the women's game, was inducted as a builder into the Hockey Hall of Fame in 2005, and currently serves as vice-president of the International Ice Hockey Federation.*

On the NHL's undeniable appetite for hyper-aggressiveness and its continued reliance on fighting as a selling point: It's very, very discouraging, to say the least. They're so slow in reacting to these things and I'm just amazed at the product they put out. In my view, every time one of those ridiculous sideshows happens, it's a forthright statement from the NHL [Board of] Governors to the public-at-large that says, "We simply have no confidence in our core product. We don't believe it's good enough to attract customers, so we must embellish it with the ridiculous sideshows just to attract interest from people."

And that's so wrong, because our game is a beautiful sports spectacle when it's presented in the way it's intended to be played and the way it's written in the rulebook. I would even go so far as to say that, if the officials called the game the way it was written in the book—and the officials will do what they are directed to do—there would actually be more contact in the game. And best of all, they would be more clean, hard, legitimate hits. Because no matter what they try and tell you, the truth is that hockey is and always will be a body-contact game.

This fear of losing the body contact is just a ridiculous argument. Everybody makes the comparison between [the NHL] and the NFL. In the NFL, if you even brush the quarterback, it's a penalty of 15 yards and a first down. End of story. That's a big penalty in that kind of game, and players do cartwheels to avoid hitting the guy who's putting on the show, and yet it still is a very physical game. Well, in [the NHL], the star player who is putting on the show, he becomes the target, and the league does nothing to properly discourage it.

On the authoritarian culture that frowns upon hockey players speaking their minds, especially when it comes to their own safety: The players can't defend themselves in this because they immediately go from tough, macho guy to wimp. If they speak up, they get ridiculed, and it's really wrong. But somebody's got to speak for the players, and I don't know where the [NHL]PA is in this. They should be loud and strong on this issue.

On the large disparity in salary between the NHL and AHL, and how that dictates a desperation on a player's behalf to play the game more aggressively than another player competing for the same job: You've got to play the game with respect, and players would want to do it right. But it's not rocket science to realize why they do what they do. The guys who are on the third or fourth line in the NHL know they're up there with limited talent, they've got to be noticed, and the difference between fifty–sixty grand to half a million a year to be a fringe player in the NHL is so vast, it's worth enough for them to do what they have to do to get noticed.

On the first rule he would implement in the NHL to improve the quality of protection players receive: I'd put in a direct head-checking rule, just as we did in the IIHF. And tell players to honor it and beware of it, and tell the officials that they'd better call it if they see it, because if they don't, they won't get further assignments. We did it overnight, and none of the guys had trouble adjusting. And now we don't have nearly the amount the NHL has. There will always be the odd one where the referee will have to make a judgment, but if you tell them to call them if they see them and err on the side of safety, they'll do what they're told.

On the NHL's status as a role model in terms of player behavior standards for the minor pro and amateur leagues: The NHL sets the tone, and that has an effect all the way down the [hockey] ranks. Because as much as we put in certification programs and rules and innovations for coaches as to how they should act, everybody is drawn to the NHL, and what they see four to five times a week and Saturday nights on *Hockey Night in Canada*, they emulate. Parents are tougher than they've ever been—they say that's part of the game, and I can't believe that's the way it is, but that's what's happening.

• • •

Keith Primeau *played 15 years in the NHL, represented Canada at the 1998 Olympic Winter Games in Nagano, Japan, and amassed 619 points in 909 career regular-season games before retiring in 2006 partly due to a string of concussions. In addition to his duties with a minor league team in Las Vegas, he has become an outspoken advocate for head injury awareness and treatment and was instrumental in creating the website http://stopconcussions.com.*

On why hockey requires a complete ban on headshots at all levels of the game: To me, all headshots are off-limits. It's so hard to decide the intent of players, but the head has to be protected at all times. Being responsible and in control of your actions is within the players' power. I tried to play my entire career fair and honest, but I would've been prepared to pay any price if there was a penalty there for playing the game a certain way.

On the need to properly care for players who've been concussed and who've been trained to play through any pain: We need to do a better job of how we handle the number of players who've been hurt. The instant it happens, how do we take the onus out of the hands out of the player who wants to compete and the organization that wants the player to compete, and still be medically responsible? That's where we need to make the strongest changes. It's the couple minutes immediately following the injury that need to be handled differently.

On the otherwise admirable quality of bravery that can be devastating to a hockey player's health: It's a thing called courage. Players play with courage; they're competitive by nature and they want to be out there. They want to play through anything that doesn't feel drastically unnatural. But we need some rules and regulations that state the obvious and that take away the gray area from players. We need to change the mentality among players and teach them that the brain is serious business and nothing to shrug off.

On the problems brought about by the post-lockout obstruction crackdown: My biggest contention when they made the rule changes coming out of the lockout was I thought they were too drastic. I thought they should've allowed the end zone battles, where you have to fight for the puck. You could still have the freedom to move through the neutral zone, but when you have freewheeling bodies all over the ice, it's a recipe for disaster. I felt that at the time and I still feel that. Is the game great? Absolutely. Is there an opportunity to scale back and adjust and slow things down a little bit? Yes, I think there is.

On his skepticism that elite players won't continue to feel as if they're bulletproof when it comes to head injuries: Don't get me wrong, anything we do proactively to help players become more aware and prepared is tremendous. My fear is the player who watches that and says to himself, "You know what, I feel bad for that guy, but that's not me, that's not going to be me." It's going to be a challenge to convince guys that, as a matter of fact, that could be them.

• • •

David Branch *has served as commissioner of the Ontario Hockey League since 1979, and since 1996, he has added the title of president of the Canadian Hockey League. Widely regarded as one of* *junior hockey's most progressive and influential minds, he has been responsible for tough rules—including a rule banning all head-shots—and suspensions aimed at curbing over-aggressive behavior.*

On the need for continued vigilance on controlling and limiting the number of headshots at all levels of the game: We have had a concussion management program in place for the past eight years, but still have concussions in our league at a rate we feel is unacceptable. Some people have made the negative comment that our rule banning headshots takes away from the physicality of the game; we've not seen that. In our view, our game still has that physical element. It's not adversely impacted on that.

Our sanctions and educational process have been significant; the latest step we're taking is an educational DVD to show all our players what a concussion really is, the symptoms, etc. That's critical. We tell players they're part of the solution to cutting down as much as possible, and we're open to all suggestions.

On the reaction his league's headshot ban received from team owners: There's complete support; I give the ownership of our teams a lot of credit. All of our owners are of the same mind and believe that we've got to see what we can do here to cut down on the injuries we're still seeing too much of. All through minor hockey, there is no such thing as a legal hit to the head. Each and every player begins the game in an environment that doesn't condone head hits.

On the NHL's insistence the junior game is less physical because of the headshot ban: There are a lot of things that are stated [at the NHL level] for convenience these days.

But diving used to be an issue in the NHL, and you hardly see any diving anymore, do you? All I can tell you is that we recognize head injuries as a problem, we're doing our best to address it, and the people associated with our league have not had a problem with the ways in which we've altered the rules to do so.

• • •

A former deputy district attorney in Los Angeles, **Allan Walsh** *has been an NHL player agent and athlete representative for 16 years, guiding the careers of some of the biggest names in the sport. In recent years he has made clear his status as a progressive voice for changing the North American game to provide a better standard of protection for his clients and all players at all levels of the sport.*

On the wide variety of player safety–enhancing changes that can be made beyond a headshot rule: There are other things beside banning hits to the head that hockey can do. The number one tweak that can be made is the hybrid no-touch icing. One thing that hasn't been talked about is going back to the pre-lockout neutral zone. There's more room in offensive zone now, and everybody's skating hard, and there's lots of corner collisions. And increased speed leads to increased collisions, while equipment resembling body armor can hurt almost as easily as it can protect.

On the lack of action on headshots by the league officials who hold the power to act: A couple of years ago, the Players' Association made a presentation to the GMs and advocated that when the blindside rule was being debated, all headshots be banned. The GMs rebuffed that presentation.

After a while, it feels like callous disregard for the well-being of the players.

• • •

Ian Laperriere, *a 15-year NHLer currently with the Philadelphia Flyers, was named the toughest player in the league by* The Hockey News *in the spring of 2010. Around the same time, he suffered a concussion during the first round of the playoffs—after taking a puck off his face—and missed the entire 2010–11 season with post-concussion symptoms. He has yet to officially retire and remained around the Flyers all year, but still had vision problems with indoor lighting. There is no guarantee the 37-year-old will ever play competitively again.*

On remaining a part of the Flyers organization despite being unable to play because of post-concussion symptoms: You want to be part of what's going on—that's the toughest part for me. I take care of myself and my body and I'm glad it's responding. But am I down? Yes. Am I depressed? No. This year, I've done a little bit of pro scouting and working with [the team's] young players in practice. The Flyers couldn't be more supportive.

On what he's learned—and how he's been frustrated—since being affected by head injuries: It is scary, but what drives me nuts is everybody in the [NHL] is talking about it, but nobody is doing anything about it. From the league's side or from the player's side.

On the drastic changes in the game since his first extended NHL stint in 1994—and on what hasn't changed: Don't get me wrong, headshots have always been part of the game. Maybe a couple years back, head hits like the ones we're seeing today would go under the radar. Hockey is a physical sport. If you want to totally get rid of headshots, just make it a no-contact game. But that won't be hockey. But it's true that, when I broke in, if there was a guy who was six-foot-five, he was a goon who couldn't skate. Now guys are huge, and they're great skaters and great hitters.

On the need to drastically ratchet up NHL supplemental discipline penalties for repeatedly over-aggressive players: I really do think the league is missing the boat on clearly bad hits that they should [punish] players with a huge amount of games. Suspending a player for a couple games won't hurt the guy. It may hurt him a bit in the wallet, but he's going to forget about that quickly. Those four-, five-, six-game suspensions don't work anymore.

With hits that are obvious, and with the repeat offender, that's the time to make a stand, put your foot down, suspend him 20 games, see who the next [player] is [who's] going to do that. There won't be one.

• • •

Alyn McCauley enjoyed a splendid junior hockey career with the Ottawa 67s, followed by a decade-long NHL career with the Toronto Maple Leafs, San Jose Sharks, and Los Angeles Kings. Unfortunately, he suffered head injuries both with the 67s and while in the professional ranks, and after a slew of injuries, played his last season in 2006–07 at the relatively young age of 30.

On what he's learned over the years since suffering his first concussion as a teenaged player in Ottawa: It scares me a lot. There was a lot I came to understand, especially after getting hit the last time [in the NHL] by [veteran defenseman] Sheldon Souray. It really opened my eyes. There were times I wasn't feeling 100 percent, got on the ice, and probably was risking a lot more than I knew I was.

At times I've been painted with a brush in terms of knowing what I'm talking about, but my reason for doing it is making players make as educated a decision as they can. There's information out there, try learning it as best you can. A lot of the times the decision is left up to the player, and the player wants to be part of the team and be back in the action. When you want to compete and the decision is placed in your hands, you don't always make the right decision.

And I played with concussion-like symptoms—they weren't strong symptoms, but they made it so you didn't feel 100 percent yourself. I went back out there because that's what I wanted to do. At the end of my life, that may have been a real tragic decision to get back out there. Who knows?

On allowing a small degree of obstruction tactics to slow down the game and potentially reduce the number of concussions suffered: The obstruction part—for me, if the rules regarding it are lessened a little bit and we lose a bit of that speed, but it's safer for the guys, that seems like a fair trade. And it seems like an easier thing than removing the instigator rule. I do think it's a good step to make players more responsible for their actions.

On the notion of keeping concussed players out of the lineup for longer to guard against late-onset symptoms and further damage suffered by players who return to action too quickly: I really like that gradual process of getting the player back onto the ice. The shortest term would be seven days—a week to make sure you're healthy. Even with an NHL schedule, you're talking three games at most that you'd be out for. That's not a lot to make sure you're healthy, not just for when you return, but for the rest of your life.

On the impact hard-shell hockey equipment has on a player's on-ice behavior: I wouldn't mind seeing some of the equipment changed. I really feel like players have such a sense of invincibility; they throw themselves at other players without any care for even their own bodies. More times than not it's the other player that gets hurt, but if you didn't have so much padding on, that sense of invincibility, you might ease up a little bit.

You look at a guy like Cal Clutterbuck—I like what he brings, but he's not a huge player. If he wears some of that equipment that was worn back in the 1980s, is he going to be that bold on the ice? Years ago, there was at least a thought a player had before he went to hit a guy. Now it really seems like there's no thought that happens before contact.

• • •

David Perron *was in his fourth season with the St. Louis Blues when the offensively talented left-winger was waylaid at center ice by a body check from San Jose Sharks star center Joe Thornton in a November 4, 2010, game—a body check that included contact with Perron's head. The 23-year-old, Sherbrooke, Que., native has not played a game since and continued to suffer post-concussion symptoms throughout the 2010–11 campaign.*

On the main message the hockey culture stresses for its best players: We're taught from a very young age to play our way through injuries. And normally, you'll play with a sore hip flexor, a sore finger, sore this and that, and you end up being fine. Something we do on a daily basis. Sometimes you'll hear a commentator say, "Oh, he's playing hurt," but after five games of the season, who isn't? By then you've got bumps and bruises all over your body. And it's not a big deal, we get used to that. But this is much different. Months and months after I was hit by Joe [Thornton], I'm still not feeling quite right.

On his feelings regarding Thornton's hit, which landed the Sharks center a two-game suspension: I've got nothing against Joe Thornton. I watched him when I was young, he's a hell of a player, and if I can play as good as him one day I'll have a good career. The play was an unusual situation in that Joe just came out of the box, and I looked back to get the pass, and he hit me. As a player, you know you have to keep your head up. I did that when I was coming up the ice; I scanned the area in front of me, and there was nobody there, so I knew I could look back and get the puck. You'd never get the pass if you couldn't see the puck; it's impossible. And as I do that, he hits me. I don't know if Joe was frustrated from the first penalty, but all I can really say is we as players need to be careful. I'm fine with Joe. I don't think he's a dirty person, but I think it was a dirty hit.

On the emotional outcry from Penguins owner Mario Lemieux after outbreaks of needless violence in the 2010–11 NHL season: Mario coming out with ideas is something I was really amazed and proud of. I thought that was really smart of him. And their GM, Ray Shero, stepping in and backing him up was great to see.

Before the last lockout, Mario talked about the NHL being a garage league with all the obstruction going on, and everybody eventually had to agree with him and the game was changed.

I think this time he's going to have the same impact. Within two or three more years, there are going to be rules on head-shots even stricter than what we have today.

On asking more from NHL players in terms of personal responsibility for their actions: Players are going to be smarter as they get used to the rule changes. If it's something that you call every time, coaches aren't going to keep scream-ing at guys to finish their check.

If the puck isn't close to a player when you hit him? I'm sorry, I know if you're right there when an opponent passes the puck, it's hard to stop that fast. But many times, I see guys on every team who can stop, but they keep going only because their role is to be physical. I don't want to take physicality out of the game, but if you have enough time to skate at a guy, you have enough time to hit him correctly. That's why I think all head hits should be banned. It doesn't matter if it's intentional or accidental—it should be like high-sticking. You have to be careful with your stick and your body.

On how the game can improve beyond its current state simply by demanding more consistency in applying rules, and by increasing the penalties for headshots: I know it's a sport and fans like to see good hits and all that, but I think the game will be even better and the hits we're going to see will be better to watch because you know guys are respecting themselves and doing things the right way.

To me, it's pretty simple. If you call everything—every late hit that's illegal, then the coaches aren't going to say, "finish every check" as much. I know what it's like when you don't finish your check sometimes; you get back to the bench and coaches tell you you've got to finish your check. We all grew up with the same mentality, and it's nothing against the coach, it's just the reality of what's allowed on the ice right now.

But if it's called on every occasion, nobody will be complaining if you pull up a little bit. Again, it's not taking the physicality of the game away; it's taking away useless hits that cause injuries we don't need. And what are you really doing by finishing your checks three seconds after the play other than hurting him? What are you trying to do? Yeah, you can intimidate him, but do it when he has the puck. If you can hit him in the right situation, you can have a great hit.

On his reaction to NHL changes that instruct teams to have doctors examine players immediately after suffering a concussion: Listen, I don't want to sound like I'm pissed off at everything. The league's changes are a positive step. But some of the things that have happened would be unpreventable even with the changes. Even if there would have been a doctor there when I was hurt, he would've sent me back out there on the ice because I felt fine during the game, but I didn't have symptoms until two days later.

On the role fighters play in the modern game, and who loses out because the role is still around: In terms of fighting, it takes value away from the players who are actually fast enough to finish checks. Guys who aren't fast enough aren't going to be able to play in the league. If you call every hit, your value is going to be higher because you're fast enough to finish your check.

If that's the case, if you can play hockey and you can make hockey plays, and the other guy who's stronger than you because he's seven inches taller and 45 pounds bigger can't skate and can't make hockey plays, that kind of player just won't be in the league.

The same goes for me—if I'm not good enough for the NHL, that's fine. But it's supposed to be the best league in the world, so you're supposed to have the best players and the best rules in the world. I want the game to be played in the best possible way.

On the farce that took place when the New York Islanders repeatedly gave ice time to American League goon Trevor Gillies in a string of 2011 game: [Gillies] got called up from the AHL, then suspended almost right away, then after he returns from suspension he does something else and is suspended again. Tell me, if the refs call everything that happens on the ice, and you're a GM, who are you going to call up first from the minors—the guy who can't keep up with the game, or the guy who's on the first line in your farm team and who knows how to play hockey with speed and skill? That's an easy call. And if you don't have those type of [enforcer] players, those incidents won't happen.

On a call-to-arms for more NHL players to speak out regarding the need for change: We need the best players in the league to come out and talk about it. I know it's probably not Sidney [Crosby's] style to come out and say all this stuff, but it's something that's going to keep happening at the end of the day. If it keeps going the way it's going, and you see the number of concussions players are suffering, you can't keep turning away from it. At least, I can't.

Look at the obstruction problem. I'm happy guys like Mario Lemieux, Brett Hull, and Jeremy Roenick spoke out about it years ago when it first became a problem and they weren't afraid to speak their mind. We're playing a better game right now because they said something, and we as players appreciate that. If I saw those guys, I would thank them.

I know some media will hear what I say and say, "He's whining," and this and that. Well, fine, I'm whining, but if in 10 years from now the game is better, the guys who are playing at that time will appreciate what we did for them. That's what it's all about.

On the severity and potential ramifications of the concussion epidemic: You don't want guys playing with a concussion. This is a life-affecting thing. It's not about hockey anymore, it's about your life. What's hockey if you turn 40 and you live until you're 80 or 90, and for 50 years you can't think properly and you don't remember your grandson's name?

When we start playing hockey, it's because we have fun doing it. When I'm five years old, I'm not thinking about making the NHL or making money by playing hockey. I'm playing to have fun, and I thought that way basically until I was 18 or 19 and playing in the NHL.

On what he sees as the core components of the game and the importance of NHL referees enforcing the rule-book: Maybe I'm different than other people, but to me, the basics of the game are the speed, the skill, and the physicality—but it all has to be applied the right way.

I think hockey referees are doing a good job for the most part. It's not an easy position to be put in. But the NFL is a good example. If you look at the games in the NFL, whether it's pre-season, regular season, or the Super Bowl, the games are all refereed the exact same way. In football, if a guy gets pushed down with two minutes left in the game or two minutes into the game, it doesn't matter—it's a five-or-10-yard penalty. And it should be the exact same way in the NHL. I know the speed is faster in the NHL than it is in the NFL and that makes it harder to officiate. But I don't know—if you need a referee in the stands to make more calls, then do it, because we'll make the game better and safer.

When the [NHL] brought a second referee on the ice, all the stuff that was going on behind the play—the slashing on the back of the legs, for example—it all stopped instantly, because there was someone to look for it and call it. You can't get away with that anymore. There's a solution to every problem, and we've just got to find it. Again, I think the league is making progress, but it's got to be something we can't give up on. We've got to keep going, and we need guys like Mario Lemieux to come out and do what they do. And I really appreciate what the media are doing to try and make that change.

On the loudest proponents of keeping fighting and hyper-aggressiveness in the game: You know what I notice? The guys getting away with cheap shots and borderline hits, late hits, and all kinds of different things, they're the ones who speak up and say, "We don't want change to happen because it will change the game."

Well, of course they don't want it to happen, because if it did, they won't be in the league anymore! Should you be in the league if you're not fast enough to get to a player and hit him cleanly?

• • •

Kerry Fraser *spent three decades as an NHL referee and became one of the most prominent and colorful NHL officials in league history. After retiring at the end of the 2009–10 season, Fraser moved to the broadcasting side of hockey and currently provides perspective on officiating for TSN and TSN.ca.*

On violence as a promoted product of hockey in North America, and what the game is losing by not addressing it: The first premise I have is that this is a hockey-cultural issue. It's not just about putting in a rule that's going to restrict a particular negative component of the game. This is cultural— it extends down to the grassroots, and the obvious premise is to have it changed and have that change come from the top and work its way down from the [NHL's] players through the junior and college systems and down to the development levels and the kids.

In my view, the solution starts with players who have been raised in this new culture of hitting that has taken some time to evolve. It's the same as when obstruction took some time to evolve before being identified as a major problem; we used to call it hooking and holding, and then it became a catchphrase locked into one basket we call obstruction. The same can be said for hits to the head; it doesn't matter if it was intentional or not, a head hit is a head hit.

Now we're trying to determine what is a legal hit to the head, and what is an illegal contact to the head. With new medical information that has come out, the factual information coming out tells us that any hit to the head, whether it's frontal, blind side, or from the back, is bad, is negative, and has the capability of causing a concussion. The NHL has tried to identify what kind of hit to the head it will allow, and what kind it won't allow. I don't think that's sound judgment. I don't think that makes sense.

We know the problem, we know the potential of the end result, so let's try and eliminate that as best we know how. From an ownership level, you want to protect the asset; if you owned a hedge fund, you'd want to protect your asset and that's what players are to the league.

The best hockey I ever saw Keith Primeau play ended with a concussion. The year before he was finished was the race Philadelphia had with Tampa in the league's semifinal [in 2004]; he won the game on his own and was dominant. And he only played a handful of games after that, in part because of head injuries. You want to see that as rarely as possible in this game, and it seems as if it's going the other direction and becoming more of a regular occurrence. If we want the sport to thrive as best it can, we can't have that.

On how NHL team owners and executives are starting to wake up to the problem of player safety, and the vested interest some franchises have in keeping the on-ice status quo: As [Carolina Hurricanes GM] Jim Rutherford, and [Buffalo Sabres GM] Darcy Regier and [Calgary Flames majority owner] Murray Edwards, and [Montreal Canadiens owner] Geoff Molson have expressed publicly the need to eliminate this kind of thing. And that exposes that the NHL owners are divided on this stuff. That's not new. You're never going to get a unanimous decision a certain way, because some teams are just built with a certain style in mind.

For example, the restraining tactics of a team that doesn't have the budget to pay a skilled player and is built instead with slow plough horses of players. Those teams wanted to slow the game down so that they could restrain skilled players—because it suited the players that they had—so certain teams always voted against any tactics intended to open the game up.

But the headshot issue is different, in that it's more of a philosophical perspective that argues that hockey is unique, is tough, is a contact sport—and if you don't like the contact, mothers, soccer moms, go let your kids play soccer instead. I don't think that is a responsible answer to address what we know today about the nature and the ramifications of head injuries. So let's work, not at reducing hits to the head, let's work at eliminating them.

On the cooperation that needs to take place in making hockey safer, and an example of what cooperation was able to achieve in regard to obstruction: It's going to take a concerted effort, not just to put in a rule and enforce it and suspend people but also to have a re-education process. The league and the NHLPA have to be involved in it and buy in. The obstruction that was eliminated in 2005 was a result of buy-ins by each party: the Players' Association, the league, the General Managers, they all said, "We're going to be responsible, and we agree that, whatever the referees call, we've empowered them to call this and we're not going to complain. We're going to support them through to the end and not backtrack one or two months in saying, 'oh, this isn't what we meant.'"

So, how do you stop it? Well, first of all, you come to an agreement, the PA and the NHL. They'll have to say, "We don't want this," or, "We only want it to this degree." That's what it comes down to: how many avoidable concussions do you want? I say, don't let them hit to the head, because we know what results when players get multiple concussions. So let's get rid of it.

So it takes the resolve to take a stand and say, number one, we want to eliminate it; and number two, how are we going to go about it? It can't just be one faction exclusively trying to get rid of this. It needs to be a joint effort.

On the adjustment process that NHL players must make to ensure fewer of them lose their careers to head injuries: It needs to be clear what players can and can't do. In addition, they need to be coached as to how they can administer a proper, acceptable check. And if they don't, the consequences must be clear. It's an education process that has to start as soon as possible, and it has to be implemented through a very quick learning curve to retool the players as far as the philosophy of checking, what's acceptable and what isn't.

The objective is to separate man from puck, not head from shoulders. All of the hits you've seen in the last few years that are in question, and many of the ones that aren't suspended or noticed, to my trained eye, happen when the players' ankles stiffen, their knees straighten, and the upper torso moves in an upward position that launches from the feet upward into the head area.

Now, [NHL Commissioner] Gary Bettman can say, "Our players don't target the head," but look at it this way: if a pitcher throws a baseball, he targets the glove of the catcher. That's where he follows through and finishes to as the target. The same thing is applying here: historically, the upper body mass was the primary target of a body check, but we're now seeing contact coming up high to the head.

So it's illogical to say they're not targeting the head, because players are following through to their target, and we can clearly see what the target is. Some may believe it could be subconscious, but that's all part of the evolution of the culture of hitting that's taken place.

On the front row seat he had watching NHL fights, and the consequences players paid for acting as enforcers: While Don Cherry or some of these other guys who I refer to as "cavemen" and the league talk about eliminating certain kinds of hits to the head, they also promote and praise players for an entirely different kind of hit to the head when they're fighting.

The fighting issue is two guys trying to knock each other out, by punching each other clearly and directly in the face and the head. We've seen [Canadian amateur player] Don Sanderson fall backwards without a helmet in a fight and die. Now, that's an isolated case, but that's the potential of what can happen.

I saw some major bouts from close proximity. I stood and watched Bob Probert. I saw a lot of his fights. When the linesman wanted to come in and stop one of Probie's fights, I watched Probie take punch after punch in the head and absorb all of them. He would wave the linesmen out, because his strategy was the old rope-a-dope where you take everything the other guy has and then unload on him when the guy was tired and he knocked him out. So you can't tell me those multiple punches to the head didn't cause the catastrophic brain disorder known as CTE [chronic traumatic encephalopathy].

And I also saw [infamous Canadiens and Maple Leafs enforcer, the late] John Kordic fight. In fact, one of the best fights I saw was a Saturday-night game in Montreal between the Canadiens and the Quebec Nordiques, and John Kordic got into a fight with Gord Donnelly, Quebec's tough guy.

It was a minute-and-a-half to two minutes of direct punches, toe-to-toe, where one guy would take the other guy's punch, not attempt to duck it, come back with another one. *Hockey Night in Canada* counted 53 direct punches to the head of one of them and about as many to the other. It was like scoring a fight card. We know what happened to John Kordic, and we know he had other problems, depression and that sort of thing. That depressive state is something I learned about when I visited the Mayo Clinic.

On the inconsistency of NHL supplementary discipline and the manner in which it affects the quality of NHL refereeing: Now we're being told the league has a hitting zone. I used to think the hitting zone was 200 [feet] by 85 [feet; the size of an NHL rink], but now there's this little space where the victim is responsible for knowing that he should be hit there. So if the victim gets hit in the head [in that zone], it's his fault.

We can't have a "hitting zone" or look for excuses as to why we can't suspend players. [Vancouver's] Raffi Torres just got off a four-game suspension heading into the playoffs, and the first check he threw was to jump at [Chicago's] Brian Campbell, a good miss, and got a two-minute charging penalty. But the next kid he leveled was [Chicago's Brent] Seabrook. He targeted his head and knocked him out, and that was deemed to be a good hockey play, with no word from [head league disciplinarian] Colin Campbell.

You can't have that. The inconsistency is what makes players and officials scratch their heads and just take their best guess and interpretation of what the league thinks.

[Tampa Bay agitator] Steve Downie probably saw the Torres hit that night, played the next night, and leaped at [Pittsburgh's] Ben Lovejoy, who saw him coming where Seabrook didn't see Torres. But think about this for a minute: Lovejoy was able to defend himself where Seabrook wasn't, and Downie didn't target Lovejoy's head, which Torres did to Seabrook.

But because Downie left his feet, that play was deemed to be a one-game suspension in the playoffs, and Torres got no supplementary discipline whatsoever. That highlights the inconsistency: the players don't know what they can and can't do; the referees see that, and they don't know what the expectation is on the calls, so when [Chicago's] Bryan Bickell takes out [Vancouver's Kevin] Bieksa in Game 6 [of the 2011 first round of the playoffs], the official thinks back in his mind, sees the Seabrook hit called a good hockey play and calls it the same way.

I'm not blaming the officials; they have to do what they're told. But there's already that feeling in the pit of the referee's stomach that he doesn't want to call a penalty that could end this game. And now there are times when he's got to go without firm, clear direction as to what he should or shouldn't be calling? That has to change.

On the ways referees dealt with the NHL's numerous attempts at getting rid of obstruction—attempts that always crumbled after an initial crackdown—before the league finally committed to changes after its 2004–05 lockout: It was frustrating back then because it was a roller-coaster ride. You sit around a table at training camp and receive direction from the league, and from that point on, there is an expectation that's placed upon yourself and all officials to carry forward the direction you've been given.

Then when the season and the roller coaster begin, you hear league people say, "Well, that's not what we meant," or, "Back off a little bit, this is more along the lines of what we intended,"—it's just another way to take your eyes off the initial direction. It defeats the purpose and takes the result you're trying to accomplish and changes it. It becomes a moving target, and it's a slide backwards.

On the April 2008 "Sean Avery Rule" playoff game between the Devils and Rangers, in which Avery faced Devils goalie Martin Brodeur at point-blank range and waved his stick in Brodeur's face (the NHL followed up the next day by rewriting its unsportsmanlike conduct penalty to include actions such as Avery's): When I watched that game, all I could think of was, "Give him an unsportsmanlike conduct [penalty]!" Avery should have received an unsportsmanlike conduct penalty, because any action designed to incite an opponent qualifies as an unsportsmanlike conduct penalty. You don't have to come up with a Sean Avery Rule, because it was already there. The referee chose not to apply it.

On the Matt Cooke blindside hit on Marc Savard, which began a run of concussions that have put Savard's career in jeopardy, and on the new rule that followed the hit, just as the Sean Avery Rule followed his incident: That's what I'm always seeing with the league—they want to write a new rule. After the terrible hit Cooke put on Savard, Colin Campbell came out and said, "The league doesn't have a rule that covers what Cooke did." I was still working for the league at the time, and I took one look at that and said, "Are you freaking serious? We don't have a rule to cover that? I've been in this league 30 years on the ice as a referee, and you're telling me there's not a rule in the book?"

In fact, there are three of them: one is called "charging"; one is called "elbowing"—because that's what it was: an elbow chicken-wing to the head; and one is called a "match penalty for an attempt to injure." Cooke was doing nothing more than to try and hurt this guy. Savard's whole body mass was exposed for him to hit, and he went after the head. So there [are] three rules that apply, and all of a sudden we have to create Rule 48 about illegal hits to the head. It makes no sense.

On the need to make the NHL's chief disciplinarian position into a disciplinary panel, with a fairer approach toward handing out suspensions and fines for over-aggressive players: It's got to be taken out of one man's decision. I've always proposed that you make it a tribunal. Have an NHLPA member on it, and have a league representative, and then bring in a neutral third party [such as a member of the International Ice Hockey Federation, or Hockey Canada/USA] who has no vested interest in either side.

And have a former referee on that tribunal. My decisions aren't always right, but at least they came out of a sense of neutrality. I might have thought a certain player acted like a jackass, but I always believed he deserved the same level of protection under the rules. That's the kind of mental approach you need for that job.

On the idea that those who criticize the NHL product and its direction hate the sport: I love the game. I know the NHL is trying to move in the right direction, but it's been slow coming, and it seems to me like they've been dragged to it, in kind of a begrudging way almost. They do studies that take forever. They do studies about how hard the equipment is, for five years anyway. But the need is there for change now. You don't need to study how hard the equipment is to know it's a problem and where it's being placed in a hit is causing the problems.

I'm very passionate about this, for the benefit of the players and the good of the game. For very factual statements I made at the Mayo Clinic [in October 2010] I was retaliated against, my credibility diminished. But nobody's trying to soften the game.

We're not talking about reduction of physicality or body checking; we're talking about an appropriate method of body checking and physicality that doesn't include the targeting or hitting of the head of an opponent. That's all. I saw hits in the 1970s, 1980s, and 1990s, but what we're seeing now, instead of the hit focusing on the body mass, we're seeing it focused on the head. Let's just bring that down below the shoulders.

On the need for NHL supplementary discipline that is more punitive than it is at present: As a referee, one of my primary objectives was to provide safety for the participants involved. That's what the rules are designed for, in part. Safety is a big issue. You can't break a stick over another guy's head and not be subject to a match penalty, and a hearing, and a suspension. But historically, the suspensions have been light—one game here, two games there—and that's just a night off for somebody. That's just a rest. If you lose 10 games of salary, or as happened in the case of [Blackhawks winger] Tom Lysiak [when Lysiak was suspended 20 games in October 1983 for intentionally tripping a linesman], if you lose 20 games of salary, then that's meaningful. That gets people's attention. And players won't do that anymore.

Anything at all that could be judged a severe enough consequence to eliminate this is worthwhile. It's ultimately about players being responsible and accountable for their actions. And if it takes making ownership and coaching accountable to help to change that, so be it.

They need to make a concerted effort, from all elements of the game, to get on the same page and determine how they're going to protect the players from themselves. The players do this because they can. Because they're allowed. Because there's no consequence for those tactics.

Remember what [San Jose Sharks winger and normally non-aggressive player] Dany Heatley did? Why would he elbow a guy in the head? He got off really lightly, because there was no hockey play there. He was intending to hurt the guy. Same with [Penguins winger and non-goon] Chris Kunitz's head hit on [Tampa Bay's] Simon Gagne, who is one concussion away from being Keith Primeau or Savard. Why would a guy do that?

The answer is, because he can. There's a minimal risk of consequence, and because it's a reflex culture of the way to hit, there's only a minimal risk for the player doing the hitting. Until it's clear, until there's not a crapshoot, roll-the-dice element players see where they feel they can take their chances on a one-or-two-game suspension, the game won't be cleared up.

• • •

Former junior hockey player and 18-year NHL player agent **Pat Brisson** *now manages the careers of numerous young stars such* *as Pittsburgh's Sidney Crosby and Chicago Blackhawks captain Jonathan Toews. Since Crosby was sidelined by a pair of concussions in January 2011, Brisson has become more informed on the issue of headshots and more vocal on the value of a complete headshot ban. He stresses that the views he expresses are his and not necessarily the views of his clients.*

On the conditions that put hockey in a position where the game has to change, and the spotlight Crosby's injury has provided for the issue: The game is much faster, the players are much stronger, and we have to look at things now to address what we're seeing and dealing with on an increasing basis. I played hockey and had a few concussions playing junior when I was young. But you see players falling like flies now. So you look at what's happening and say there's got to be a need for another adjustment.

The problem is, though players are bigger and faster and check harder, the brain is still the same size. And it's the brain we're talking about and should be most concerned about. If you have a tear in your knee, you can fix it and walk again without any problem. But the brain is so complicated, and that's why we still have trouble defining what a mild concussion is versus a more serious concussion.

Of course, when something happens to Sidney Crosby, the concussion issue is going to be magnified. But when you go to a movie, you look to see who is in it, right? But the bottom line is that all the players, whether you're a player on a two-way contract, a fourth-line winger, or a seventh D, it doesn't matter. Many players are being affected, not just Sidney. I do believe in the old days a lot of players were concussed and played while they were concussed. But when someone like that goes down, lots of questions need to be answered.

On the opposition, inside hockey's corridors of power, toward the rapid change and response—including a headshot ban—needed for dealing with head injuries: It's hard to view things in other ways sometimes, because we grew up with certain traditions and a cultural way of looking at things. But we have to learn how to put ourselves a little outside of the box sometimes.

Some hockey establishment people will come in not so much with an arrogance but with the attitude that, "Hey, this is the way the game is played and if you want to play it, this is how you play it." Well, let's be logical here. Let's try to analyze it.

All I'm suggesting is that, in the near future, when the league and players get together to talk, they look at the headshots issue like they looked at high-sticking. It's not fair to referees, with the speed you see the game played at, to try and judge intent. It's not going to slow down the game. If anything, guys will be compelled to avoid giving those hits and to be aware, because they won't want to be suspended.

And all this talk that the game will have physicality removed if we ban headshots? Listen, players will find a way to be competitive and still be physical. If suspensions are strict, players will find a way to compete without getting themselves in trouble with the league. If a player is suspended six, seven, or even 10 games instead of two or three games, and instead of paying $20,000 in fines they're paying $100,000, believe me, things will change. But they're still going to be aggressive and competitive, because they have to win.

On the changing attitudes of NHL owners, team general managers, and players to the concussion problem: I've had a lot of discussions with owners in the past six months and, I must admit, in my opinion things are changing a lot. They're looking like this as, "I'm losing an asset." If I lose a Jonathan Toews or a Sidney Crosby or Nashville loses Matthew Lombardi, they're realizing how important an asset they're going without.

So more and more teams are telling their general managers how they feel. And I think that's something that's going to continue to happen as players learn more about this issue. [Penguins GM] Ray Shero has a good voice, and he uses it very well. He had a message from his owner to deliver [i.e., that Lemieux was no longer willing to tolerate predatory behavior], but Ray was totally on board with it. And more and more teams are seeing it that way.

That's why I'm encouraged. I told some of our players who are in favor of abolishing headshots and being extremely severe on players who deliver them, I said, "Guys, be patient. It's not a question of five or 10 years from now, it's more a matter of a year or two, and maybe months before we see positive change."

I would say as far as the awareness and willingness to want to do more regarding headshots and concussions—60 to 70 percent of my clients are now in that group. And it might have been at 40 percent two or three years ago. At the beginning of the season during training camp, teams are exposing players to substance and abuse programs, then a DVD about how to play the game properly. And sometimes the player's attention span can wander and messages don't sink in. But once players are going through the season and seeing so many injuries, more are very concerned with the problem.

I want to be cautiously optimistic that the league is doing the right thing, but I also want to encourage players to speak their minds. Speak to [NHLPA executive director] Donald Fehr. Talk to the Players' Association. Talk to your teammates and your peers. And I like what the league did with setting up a panel of [former NHL stars Rob] Blake, [Steve] Yzerman, [Joe] Nieuwendyk, and [Brendan] Shanahan; those guys understand the game, have played it before and after the lockout and the obstruction changes. And they can speak to players, and players can get answers.

On Mario Lemieux's suggestion to fine team owners for suspendable acts committed by their players: An organization can only manage so much. If I'm a player, at the end of the day, no matter which team I'm playing for, if I'm on the third line and my job is to be aggressive and finish my checks, that's what I have to do. But if it's going to cost me to put my elbow high too many times, if it's going to cost me a 10-game suspension instead of a two-game suspension, I'm not going to do that. So personally, I don't see that idea as more of a solution than the personal responsibility players have.

On the effect concussions are having on the amateur levels of hockey: Concussions at the pro level are one thing, but it does also affect the lower levels. The NHL is the role model as to how things should be done. And no matter what, what they do has an effect on other leagues.

The guy you pay $35 to to referee a bantam game, he'll look at himself when he's out there calling a game as if he was [veteran NHL referee] Bill McCreary or Steve Walkom doing it. And if the Steve Walkoms of the world are told to have a more rigid way of policing the game, it's going to have an effect on the lower levels.

Sometimes I close my eyes at midget games because it's so scary what's going on out there. But you follow your role models, and that's the NHL. The NHL is a league the youngsters are looking up to the NHL.

FIGHTING ON

10 THOUGHTS AND SUGGESTIONS FOR THE FUTURE

As can be seen throughout this book, a romanticized, cavalier lack of regard for hockey player safety has been a key component of the North American game for the past century. And although a significant portion of the hockey-watching population in Canada and the United States has been persuaded the current state of the game represents the sport at its best, the opposite is true.

We discover more and more each day that hockey players are being decimated, physically and psychologically, beyond the wildest fears of anyone associated with the sport. The damage is being suffered by both professional players at the highest levels of the game, as well as by amateurs who will only be able to dream of competing in the National Hockey League.

In addition, hockey's image continues to be sullied by the tacit endorsement of over-aggressive athlete behavior and self-policing among the players—and the game pays a high price for it in terms of recruiting future athletes. Today's parents thinking of entrusting their children to hockey need only see one televised "highlight" of a player being carried off the ice on a stretcher before seeking out another sport in which to invest their emotions, time, and money.

Making matters worse, hockey's gatekeepers have failed to treat the issue of player safety with the gravity it deserves. When the NHL's powers-that-be are confronted with questions about the issue of safety in the workplace, they either react at a sloth-like pace to address the problem, or they turn antagonistic toward the questioners and huffily instruct nonbelievers to take their passion elsewhere.

Thankfully, time has proven to have a way of pushing all aspects of society, sports included, toward a more progressive end. At one point in NHL history, those who advocated in favor of mandatory goalie masks and helmets for skaters were labeled as soft and promptly dismissed. But the world changed and the game had to change with it, and now the hockey world readily accepts both goalie masks and player helmets as necessary to playing the sport.

The same was true when the NHL decided to clamp down once and for all on the clutch-and-grab Dead Puck Era. Hockey's conservative element claimed that boring, constant scrums and a fixation on containing talent rather than accentuating it was to the sport's benefit. It was anything but, making the game all but unwatchable. But people still spoke out against it, tolerance for it lessened, and, eventually, the sport shifted focus and improved.

That's what we're looking at today when it comes to violence in hockey. It is a problem that has been allowed to fester for too long and the game is worse off for it, but attitudes toward it among the players and public are changing—and with it, the thirst for an adjustment in the sport is on the rise.

Each subsequent medical study that will be issued long after this book goes to press will only confirm how desperately hockey requires a smarter, safer approach if its players are to enjoy productive lives away from the rink. And as that process plays out, more people each day will come to terms with what hockey was, is, and has to be if it's going to continue capturing the hearts, and minds (and disposable incomes) of future generations.

As a final summation, let's recap five main areas to focus on when deciphering whether hockey is headed in the right direction:

1. Changes in Culture

By far the most important area in need of change, North American hockey culture has to get past its deep-rooted dependence on players hitting to hurt, as opposed to players hitting to separate their opponent from the puck. This is a subtle, but crucial, difference—one that must be emphasized beyond any other principle.

You do that only through a total re-education process, starting at the NHL level and descending through amateur programs. If it only happens from the amateur level without total buy-in from the pros, what exactly are hockey programs saying to young players and their parents?

Are they saying that the better a child gets at the sport and the more he rises through the ranks of the amateur game, the more risk he puts himself in? That if the kid is talented and hardworking enough and beats the odds to earn an NHL job, his head and body and overall well-being become legitimate targets for some over-excited, borderline AHLer who will do anything to keep a well-paying job?

If we're being honest with ourselves, we have to admit that's precisely what the game is telling people today. North American hockey is saying to them, "talent can be a blessing on the ice, but a curse everywhere else," and people are supposed to sit there and accept that as they and/or their loved ones are subjected to potentially life-changing injuries, all for someone's entertainment?

Hockey simply can't afford that perspective any longer. And rooting out that attitude over time means confronting hockey's pervasive and predominant revenge/retribution culture head-on. It means changes to NHL hockey telecasts, intermission shows, and TV highlight packages—including an end to the sensationalist junking-up of the game through fighting—and embracing a shift to promote the sport's core qualities of speed, skill, and *acceptable/responsible* body checking.

More importantly, professional players must better appreciate the place of their hockey career in the overall scope of their lives. Too often you hear a player echo the words of Dallas Stars enforcer Krys Barch, who said on Twitter that he and other NHLers make the trade-off of money and competitiveness early in life in exchange for the risk of a lesser quality of life in their seventies and beyond.

But as we're starting to see now, NHL players' quality of life can be adversely affected long before a player makes it to his seventh decade. He could be in his forties, like poor Bob Probert was before he died suddenly. Or he could be struggling before he makes it to his thirtieth birthday—like Derek Boogaard, who was 28 when he died. Or he could be battling years after he retires from the game, as Jim Thomson did before achieving sobriety only recently.

Hockey players need to believe in their worth as individuals and as a collective group of irreplaceable talent far more than they do at present. And when the day arrives where NHLers no longer subserviently act out management's battle plans and put a higher value on their lives away from the arena, hockey will be in a much better place—and the other elements necessary to a safer environment will fall into place that much easier.

2. Changes in Equipping Players and Arenas

Undoubtedly, hockey players have benefited from advances in protective equipment. But along with providing a better sense of security from rapidly moving sticks, pucks, and bodies, improved equipment also has raised the invincibility factor among athletes.

At the professional levels, this has resulted in players literally launching themselves into the opposition as human projectiles—and the equipment of the over-aggressive player/launcher is doing about as much physical damage as anybody's body bulk or muscle. Former NHL veterans from bygone eras will tell you they could not afford to play that way, because they would have suffered nearly as much damage to their own bodies as the players they would have been recklessly careening into.

Nobody is touting a return to the days of chest protectors that looked like they were made out of egg cartons and elbow pads that looked like thimbles attached to rubber bands. However, if players are to understand that their physical person can inflict major and lasting damage to another competitor, they need to feel the repercussions in their bones, and you can't do that with hard-shell plastic covering key parts of their bodies.

At the same time, the quality and design of NHL arenas also has proven to have an effect on player safety. Until the end of the 2010–11 season, the league still had six arenas with "seamless glass" boards systems—a rigid, punishing design that doesn't allow players to easily absorb hits as happens with the more widely used flexible boards/glass system. The NHL made clear its intent to force the remaining six seamless glass arenas to change for the 2011–12 campaign. But that doesn't mean there's no opportunity to look at each of the league's 30 rinks and pinpoint problem areas that need to be changed.

For example, not until Canadiens forward Max Pacioretty suffered a severe injury in 2011 after striking his head on one of the iron stanchions in Montreal's Bell Centre did the Centre install additional padding on all of the stanchions. In all likelihood, there are more ways the NHL and the rest of the hockey world could re-imagine aspects of arena design and safety standards. But it will take a league with an honest interest in improving player protection to sniff out and accept those new ideas.

So far, the NHL has yet to demonstrate that honest interest.

3. Changes in Rules and the Interpretation of the Rulebook

There are numerous rules that could be altered to improve the overall well-being of hockey players. At the NHL level, for instance, visors could be made mandatory (or ushered in more slowly via a grandfather clause) in the blink of an eye, just as no-touch icing or a hybrid thereof could be implemented at any point in time. All that's needed to do so is the political will from NHL team owners and/or management executives to make those changes.

But beyond the idea of adding new rules, there is a concept equally crucial to curbing wanton violence and assorted idiocy on hockey rinks: simply have officials stop selective interpretation of the regulations and instead call the rulebook in its present form.

As veteran NHL referee Kerry Fraser noted, the league instructs its officials on the style of game it wants called during each season and the officials do their best to follow orders. If they're told to take a harsher view of after-the-whistle shenanigans and scrums, they'll do just that. If they are directed to send more players to the penalty box for the slashing and assorted stickwork hockey people predict would follow a fighting crackdown, the officials will do that as well.

But at the risk of repeating a theme, the real power here lies in the hands of NHL team owners. They are the ones who tell NHL's Gary Bettman what to do, the ones who get to decide what is and isn't tolerable behavior inside their buildings. It's the owners who must be willing to stand up for their employees (aka their players), the owners who have to shut their mouths when one of their own players (be he a superstar or fourth-liner) commits an act of aggression and is assessed a game misconduct, fine, and/or suspension.

Hockey's rules aren't handed down from generation to generation like a scimitar. The game has not always been played in one particular manner. The rulebook is an organic, evolving document that can be added to, but that often has a rule in place to deal with a seemingly new on-ice problem.

And like any document, it is only as powerful and effective as the person holding it wishes it to be.

4. Changes in Supplemental Discipline for Over-Aggressive Play

Although the NHL appeared to address widespread criticism of its ludicrous and unjustifiable player discipline process in early June 2011—including the changing of the guard at the top when Colin Campbell left the job of chief disciplinarian and was replaced by former star winger Brendan Shanahan—there was no guarantee the league had turned a corner and finally was applying a uniform standard of punishment for all its players.

Indeed, in the months leading up to Campbell stepping down, the NHL had announced tweaks to its concussion treatment protocol while reiterating its message that it would be doing its best to cut down on head injuries whenever possible. Yet shortly after that announcement, San Jose Sharks star winger Dany Heatley blatantly threw an elbow at Dallas Stars agitator Steve Ott, and Heatley received only a two-game suspension—about the same supplemental penalty players in the years before him would have received for a similar act.

Not only did the feeble slap on Heatley's wrist reinforce the notion that the NHL wasn't serious about taking a tougher approach to head injuries but it also gave credence to those who theorize there are two systems of justice for NHLers: one for third- and fourth-line working stiffs and enforcers, and one for the league's more talented players.

So, in spite of the fact that Bettman and the NHL were being praised in many media corners for ostensibly replacing Campbell with the well-liked Shanahan (and creating something very progressive-sounding in a "Department of Player Safety"), discerning observers are holding back on showering them with any accolades until such time as they see the league match its rhetoric with tangible action demonstrating its grave concern. As the hockey world saw during repeated failed attempts at an obstruction crackdown before the NHL finally wisened up and followed through, it is best to see real action from the league before trusting that you're guaranteed to see it.

Only when the NHL has consented to a fully transparent discipline process—featuring automatic punishments for egregious acts—will players, coaches, and organizations learn they can no longer get away with the things they once did.

Moreover, many in the hockey world have suggested the NHL do away with discipline doled out by individuals, preferring that a panel of hockey experts agree on appropriate fines and suspensions for those on-ice actions that require disciplining. Such a method would forever end the accusations of bias and subjectivity that Campbell and his predecessors have had to unfairly endure—reason enough for the league to implement.

The less the hockey media and fans have to focus on the obvious deficiencies of the NHL's supplemental discipline department, the more they can devote their attentions to the game itself.

5. Fighting

Finally, there is the most obvious barometer of the sport's evolution: the acceptance of bare-knuckle fighting, as former NHL enforcer Jim Thomson and others call it.

Just after the 2004–05 lockout season, *The Hockey News* published a cover story whose headline—"Death of the Enforcer?"—was a growing question among the hockey community. In the newer, faster, more skill-oriented NHL, fighting numbers had dropped drastically and people were asking what exactly the big, lumbering fellows who couldn't skate or score were doing taking up space on the end of a bench.

That issue of *The Hockey News* also became a rallying point for enforcers themselves; tough guys such as Georges Laraque realized they had to justify their collective existence before the importance of the position evaporated in the minds of the ticket-buying public. And so GMs began lobbying the NHL to take a step back from a philosophy that was intended to punish repeat-offense fighters by way of the instigator rule. After enough pressure was applied, the league took that backward step in February 2007; instead of assessing an automatic two-game suspension to any player (read: enforcer) who received three instigator penalties, the NHL now would wait until a player had received five instigator penalties.

In other words, after an initially progressive-sounding rule was put in place, NHL players—no, make that *goons*—received not less, but more leeway from the league to conduct their illegal business. Does that sound like an umbrella group of owners that is ready to alter their game for the better by doing away with an unnecessary aspect of the sport? Not to me, it doesn't.

To me, the NHL establishment still isn't prepared to do what is both right and necessary regarding fighting. As I wrote earlier in this book, I don't think fights ought to or can be banned, but there are many measures that can be taken to drastically mitigate against the number of all-but-staged, Dancing Bear fights we see too often.

The NHL could come out tomorrow and announce that, effective immediately, any player involved in a fight will be ejected for the remainder of the game. And the only effects that would have on the on-ice product is that: (a) goons no longer would be able to fight twice in the same contest; and (b) any other player involved in fisticuffs looking to avenge a beating in the first fight wouldn't get the opportunity.

That's one way to address fighting that instantly gives the league added credibility among other sports administrators and the general public and media; if you fight, you're out of the game, just as it is in every other organized major sport. However, the league could go even further and have a better impact on hockey's future.

In addition to automatic ejections, the NHL could announce a guaranteed minimum suspension period that changes based on the number of fights a player engages in over the course of a season. In doing so, the league could deliberately eliminate the one-trick-pony enforcer-type who too often is the NHLer most in need of policing.

With both of those rules in place—automatic ejections and sliding-scale suspensions—the NHL would be a significantly safer place to play. There would still be fights to excite fans of punching, but players would choose to enter into fights much more judiciously. And by punishing players appropriately for other acts of aggression, players would have less need to settle matters with their fists.

That seems like a happy medium to me—and a vast improvement on the Wild West attitude that passes for NHL sanity these days.

If the NHL can't even drag itself to achieving a compromise solution—if it insists on stubbornly clinging to a bygone method of conflict resolution whose ramifications affect amateurs and professionals alike—we'll know the wrong people remain in charge. And if that's the case, hockey will continue to stripped—bit by bit—of its best attributes, until its only remaining fans are those who value hard-core violence.

• • •

In closing, I want to alert you to a piece of news that may have flown underneath your radar. It was a public relations e-mail I received from the Pittsburgh Penguins, touting the organization's 2011 youth summer hockey camps.

The headline of the e-mail—the main message—read: "PENGUINS SUMMER YOUTH HOCKEY CAMP PARTICIPANTS CAN REGISTER FOR FREE BASELINE CONCUSSION TESTING."

Now, I don't want to seem ungrateful to the Penguins for making an honest effort to help identify and treat head injuries as they have. More teams ought to follow in their footsteps and protect young players as best they can. But that's the point, isn't it? Amateur hockey programs are now promoting free baseline concussion testing, as if it were some attractive selling point to parents and kids. The creation of a chart to map your cognitive destruction is now part of the publicity package. Let that sink in for a couple seconds.

That's where hockey is as a sport. But the sport won't be there much longer. It will either recognize its true strengths, change for the better and thrive, or it will continue eating its young until there aren't any more young to eat.

Free baseline concussion testing for kids. My god. Tell me again—why are we letting a sport we love do this to people we love?

ACKNOWLEDGMENTS

The opportunity to write this book came as a result of other opportunities and inspirations provided to me along the way, and I would like to thank a few people for them.

Thanks to Jason Kay, current editor-in-chief of *The Hockey News*, for giving me a platform as a hockey columnist and support for positions with which he didn't always agree, and for his guidance and friendship. Thanks to Steve Dryden, former THN editor-in-chief, for giving me my first real journalism job and providing the ultimate example of dedication and professionalism.

Thanks to all the people I've worked with at THN over the last decade-plus, including former art director Jamie Hodgson; publisher Caroline Andrews; former writers Mike Brophy and Mark Brender, and current senior writer Ken Campbell; former editors Sam McCaig, Dirk Soeterik, and Jeff Mackie; designer Erika Vanderveer; managing editor Edward Fraser and senior editor Brian Costello; writers/editors Ryan Dixon and Ryan Kennedy; web editor Rory Boylen; marketing specialists Janis Davidson Pressick, Carlie McGhee, and Alyson Young; and former THN publishers Gerald McGroarty and Wayne Karl.

Thanks to my agent, Arnold Gosewich, for persistently urging me to write this book, and to everyone at John Wiley & Sons— including my editor, Karen Milner, and publicity expert Erin Kelly—for their expert assistance in shaping the final product.

Thanks to my grandfather, David Dingwall, who encouraged me to read, look out at the world in wonder, and question it all.

Thanks to my mom, Avril Proteau, for a love words aren't equipped to describe and a heart like a tiger's.

And thanks to TB: the first and best, as always.

INDEX